Reading, Learning, Teaching

Margaret Atwood

confronting the Text, confronting the World

P. L. Thomas
General Editor

Vol. 6

PETER LANG
New York • Washington, D.C./Baltimore • Bern
Frankfurt am Main • Berlin • Brussels • Vienna • Oxford

P. L. Thomas

Reading, Learning, Teaching
Margaret Atwood

PETER LANG

New York • Washington, D.C./Baltimore • Bern
Frankfurt am Main • Berlin • Brussels • Vienna • Oxford

Library of Congress Cataloging-in-Publication Data

Thomas, P. L. (Paul Lee).
Reading, learning, teaching Margaret Atwood / P. L. Thomas.
p. cm. — (Confronting the text, confronting the world; v. 6)
Includes bibliographical references.
1. Atwood, Margaret Eleanor, 1939– —Study and teaching.
2. Atwood, Margaret Eleanor, 1939– —Criticism and interpretation. I. Title.
PR9199.3.A8Z925   813'.54—dc22   2007001092
ISBN 978-0-8204-8671-0
ISSN 1556-8288

Bibliographic information published by **Die Deutsche Bibliothek**.
Die Deutsche Bibliothek lists this publication in the "Deutsche
Nationalbibliografie"; detailed bibliographic data is available
on the Internet at http://dnb.ddb.de/.

Cover design by Lisa Barfield

The paper in this book meets the guidelines for permanence and durability
of the Committee on Production Guidelines for Book Longevity
of the Council of Library Resources.

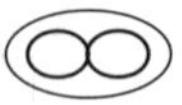

© 2007 Peter Lang Publishing, Inc., New York
29 Broadway, 18th floor, New York, NY 10006
www.peterlang.com

Printed in the United States of America

Table of Contents

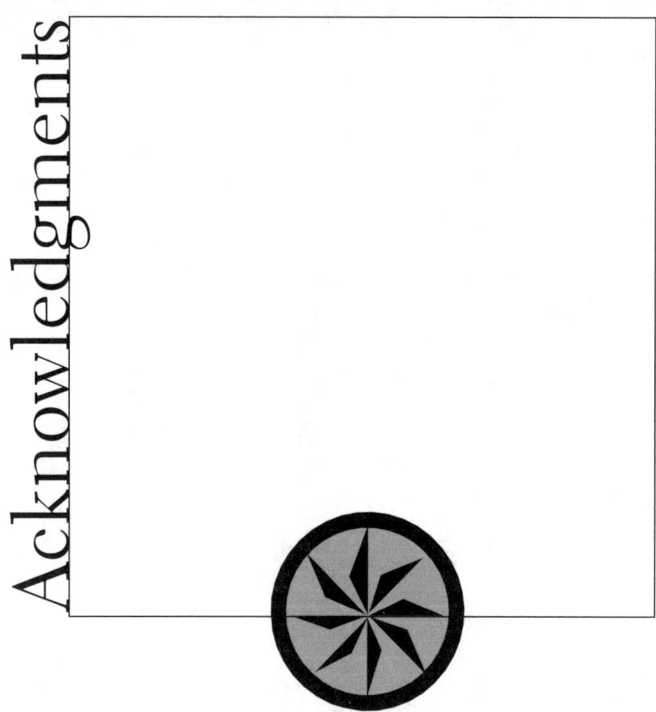

Acknowledgments

This is my third volume in this series, a series dedicated to offering writers who are confrontational in their writing and in their themes to readers, students, and teachers. As I have said before, it takes more than one person to write any book because that book is the result of everything that comes before it in that writer's life.

When I began this book on Margaret Atwood, I could not have imagined the scope of the project; I had thought that Kurt Vonnegut's canon was as much as I would ever face, but Atwood has proved to be even more overwhelming. As I wrote, she published at least four books while I was working diligently to do her existing works justice.

Those who I wish to acknowledge and thank include:

- All the students I taught at Woodruff High School from the early 1980s until the turn of the twenty-first century—especially those students in the courses where we read and discussed Atwood. I thought of them often as I wrote.
- The support of Peter Lang USA—Phyllis Korper, Bernadette Shade, and many others.
- Nita Schmidt, colleague, friend, and fellow lover of literature.
- Joe Kincheloe, who inspires me.
- The faculty and staff of the Education Department and the university at Furman.
- Family (Fran and Jessi, parents, and all), friends, colleagues, and students who are too numerous to name but invaluable to a writer and teacher.
- The brilliance of Margaret Atwood.

Confronting Nowhere, Confronting Everywhere

In her "When Afghanistan Was at Peace" (*Writing with Intent,* 2005), Margaret Atwood ends her essay musing over her visit to Afghanistan and the possibility that the trip colored her writing of *The Handmaid's Tale:* "Would I have written the book if I never visited Afghanistan? Possibly. Would it have been the same? Unlikely" (p. 207). And this is how I see my having read and re-read the works of Atwood. She—among a very few other writers—has profoundly shaped who I am as a person, a writer, and a teacher.

When composing earlier volumes in this series on Barbara Kingsolver and Kurt Vonnegut, I consciously framed each writer as being much more than the single work for which each writer is best known—*The Poisonwood Bible* for Kingsolver and *Slaughterhouse-Five* for Vonnegut. But with Atwood, I cannot hide that my anchoring work happens to be her most recognized novel, *The Handmaid's Tale.* While I will also strive to show that Atwood is much more (much, much more) than one novel, I suspect that I will come back to this monumental work many times.

The Handmaid's Tale is a brilliant work that moves the reader, but for me as a teacher it is the ideal work of literature for the purposes of learning and growing in courses that focus on students as readers and writers. The novel is a nearly inexhaustible tour de force of craft and ideas that can fuel an entire course. I am convinced that the wide range of other works offered by Atwood has the same power and potential for our English classes.

• • •

Many years ago, I sat with my Advanced Placement English and Literature class discussing the poetry they had read the night before. This particular day comes easily to mind because I began telling the class the most outlandish, most unsupportable interpretations of one poem that a reasonable person could fabricate.

The students obediently jotted down most of what I said in the margins of their textbooks. Not a single question. Not a single challenge.

The next day I confessed and asked why no one had said a word in protest. Possibly more troubling than their silence and compliance the day before was their inability even to explain their own intellectual passivity. This group was very bright and exceptionally literate, but they were also *good students.*

In American classrooms, good students are nothing if not compliant—very quiet and very eager to absorb in order to repeat the required answers when requested. In my more cynical moods, I refer to many seasoned students as "intellectual zombies," and I blame many of our traditional practices in schools for the condition— not the nature of children, not the deterioration of culture. And therein lies the motivation for this book.

While many aspects of American education have remained virtually unchanged for over a century, teachers today do face a certain raised intensity concerning some of the more harmful practices— prescriptive lesson planning, teacher-centered instruction, high-stakes testing, national and state standards, and potentially catastrophic accountability measures. Because of federal mandates such as No Child Left Behind (NCLB), our schools are often hostile to the genuine pleasure, passion, and uncertainty that can and should accompany teaching and learning, particularly teaching and learning with literature. Above all else, our schools value compliance by both teachers and students. There are to be no confrontations among people—or among ideas.

Yet if literature (all art, in fact) is anything, it is *confrontational.* Kafka (1979), in a letter to Oskar Pollak, wrote that "[a] book must be the axe for the frozen sea inside us" (p. 290). For him, literature confronted the paralysis that life imposed on him. Interestingly, Ernst Pawell (1984) states simply about Kafka: "He hated school" (p. 26). For me, there is a profound connection here. Our traditional approaches to school— stressing standardization, silence, analysis, quantification, and objectivity—work directly in opposition to the very nature of literature, the heart of English classrooms, confrontation. Kafka's metaphor of the frozen sea fits well the belief I hold about the nature of Self and of teaching and learning; the sea is an ever-moving, ever-evolving thing that is defined by its movement and constant change. Once frozen, it loses its nature.

This book will offer an opportunity for teachers and students to *confront* "the frozen sea inside us," inside our schools, and inside our literature and writing curriculums through the varied writing of Atwood. Literature can restore life and living to the classroom and to both teachers and students. Those encounters will take the form of confronting assumptions about learning theory and educational psychology in general along with reading, literature, writing, instruction, and assessment within the classroom. But I will also ask teachers and students to confront the world, to confront concepts often held so sacred that they are never reconsidered and thus allowed to wilt— capitalism, democracy, freedom, ecology, war, peace, human dignity and more, for example. Teachers will be confronting what they teach and how they teach as well (See the Introduction and Appendix of *Reading, Learning, Teaching Barbara Kingsolver,* 2005).

•••

"Inertia is my constant companion, procrastination my household pet. If I'm not eager and keen and resolved and strenuously bent, I find it very difficult to write at all," explains Atwood (2005) in the Introduction to *Writing with Intent* (p. xvii). For the teacher or professor, the wide array of works and genres offered by Atwood is both a blessing and a curse. In the following chapters I attempt to provide ample introductory discussions to most of Atwood's works, but much will be touched on briefly and some will be necessarily omitted in those discussions.

Chapter One offers a broad introduction to Atwood's life, her large body of works, and the stylistic and thematic patterns that characterize her work. Fortunately, many wonderful scholarly works are available, including biography, to assist teachers who wish to look more deeply at Atwood and her writing.

Atwood has produced a powerful and substantial body of nonfiction books since 1972, beginning with *Survival.* In Chapter Two, I explore bringing the nonfiction of Atwood into our high school and college classrooms as models for the writing of our students but also as rich literature to be considered by our students as evolving readers and critics. One strong aspect of Atwood's nonfiction for our English classes is her persistent concern for the artist, specifically the writer. Her discussions about being a writer and growing as a writer are ideal for the English classroom.

Since Atwood is most well known as a novelist, I deal with her novels in Chapters Three, Four, and Five. Chapter Three will discuss her earlier novels—*The Edible Woman* (1969), *Surfacing* (1972), and *Lady Oracle* (1976). Her central work may fairly be considered *The Handmaid's Tale* (1985), which is a brilliant work in the speculative dystopian tradition of novels. Along with a later work, *Oryx and Crake* (2003), *Life Before Man* (1979), and *Bodily Harm* (1981), Chapter Four will explore her dystopian works.

Her later novels—*Cat's Eye* (1989), *The Robber Bride* (1993), *Alias Grace* (1996), *The Blind Assassin* (2000), and *The Penelopiad* (2005)—represent the world of Atwood after her fame and critical acclaim expanded beyond her Canadian borders with the success of *The Handmaid's Tale* (including her best-selling novel to date, *Oryx and Crake,* which I discuss in Chapter Four). Chapter Five focuses on a few of these wonderful and rich works, but her later novels are all ideal for the English classroom as well-crafted novels with engaging and complex themes and styles.

Atwood's fictional publications also include several books of short stories, which are examined in Chapter Six along with a discussion of our students writing their own original stories. Atwood has published an impressive body of poetry since the early 1960s; Chapter Seven considers the poetry of Atwood and our students as poets. The final chapter touches briefly on children's literature in the Atwood catalog; Chapter Eight argues for expanding what types of works we bring into our classroom and what we assume about the nature of literature.

Woven through the chapters are related approaches to Atwood—**Entry Points** and **Connections**. Entry Points offer brief works such as poems, songs, essays, and short stories that can serve to open a lesson or unit on a longer or related Atwood work. Connections provide examples of related works (novels, essays, short stories, poems, movies) that can be taught in conjunction with Atwood, as part of a larger unit including Atwood, or as a follow-up unit.

Margaret Atwood

A Life Formed with Scissors and Matches

In *The Tent,* Margaret Atwood (2006) offers,

> I'm working on my own life story. I don't mean I am putting it together;
> no, I'm taking it apart. It's mostly a question of editing. . . . That was
> before I discovered the virtues of scissors, the virtues of matches. (p. 4)

I, on the other hand, am putting things together in this first chapter, where I will share a brief biography of a highly prolific and gifted writer, an outline of her major works in many genres (novels, nonfiction, poetry, short fiction, and an assortment of other works), a discussion of her primary thematic concerns, a consideration of her tools and techniques as a writer, and an assortment of additional avenues for understanding Atwood more fully.

I hope my piecing together will provide a solid foundation for the rest of this book as well as present an introductory argument that many of Atwood's works are ideal sources of the types of reading and writing lessons we want and need to bring into our classrooms when we seek to empower students by asking them to confront texts, notably texts that confront the world.

A Life—Woman, Writer, Canadian

While some argue that interpretation should be limited to the words on the page, the New Criticism approach to literary analysis most common in our classes, I have always found that readers, teachers, and students who know the writer's life well have a real advantage when faced with that writer's body of work. Cooke (2004) offers an excellent reason to be familiar with Atwood's life. Atwood's gift grows from her ability to deal with important themes "by making them personal, sometimes so idiosyncratically personal that they are funny," explains Cooke (p. 1)—adding a quote from Atwood's *Second Words:* "Writers are eye-witnesses, I-witnesses" (1982, p. 203).

Margaret Eleanor Atwood was born November 18, 1939, and would become both Margaret Atwood, the writer, and Peggy, the woman. Born in Ottawa, Ontario, to Carl Edmund and Margaret Dorothy, she had two siblings—Harold Leslie, born in 1937, and Ruth Kathleen, born in 1951. Since Margaret's father was a zoology professor, the family was often on the move. Until 1970, Margaret lived throughout Canada with two short periods in Boston. From 1970 until today, she has lived in England and Germany, although Canada, specifically Toronto, remains her primary residence.

Cooke (1998) describes Atwood's education as beginning informally during her childhood, specifically through her early and persistent fascination with books (including comic books, reflecting her interests as a visual artist and a writer). The young Atwood was a voracious reader and a budding artist (her fascination with comics continues); in the eighth grade she began to excel in science and English. Atwood was raised in a scientific home, where religion was not a significant part of the family but questions and skepticism were. Her family was clearly not in the mainstream of Canadian society, setting the stage for Atwood's unique perspectives.

After secondary school, Atwood pursued higher education—Victoria College, University of Toronto, B.A., 1961; Radcliffe College, A.M., 1962; Harvard University, 1962–63, 1965–67 (where she eventually chose not to finish her advanced degree). Atwood's formal education had profound influences on her writing, especially in terms of the sexism she experienced in her courses and degree programs, but ultimately Atwood embraced her life as an artist at the expense of her life as a scholar. Nonetheless, Atwood has spent a great deal of her professional life teaching as well:

- Lecturer in English, University of British Columbia, Vancouver, 1964–65;
- Instructor in English, Sir George Williams University, Montreal, 1967–68;
- University of Alberta, 1969–70;
- Assistant Professor of English, York University, Toronto, 1971–72;
- Writer-in-Residence, University of Toronto, 1972–73;
- M.F.A. Honorary Chair, University of Alabama, Tuscaloosa, Alabama, 1985;
- Berg Chair, New York University, 1986;

- Writer-in- Residence, Macquarie Univ., Australia, 1987;
- Writer-in-Residence, Trinity Univ., San Antonio, Texas, 1989.

Atwood married Jim Polk in 1968, divorcing in 1973. Later, she married author Graeme Gibson; they have three children—their daughter, Eleanor Jess Atwood Gibson, and two sons from Gibson's earlier marriage, Matt and Grae. During this active and vibrant life, she has written over fifty books. Let's now turn to the patterns of her life that appear to be most significant to the writer Margaret Atwood.

One pattern of Atwood's writing life is her discomfort with labels, her discomfort with holding up a magnifying glass to the writer's life as if that matters more than the writer's words. In her *Second Words,* Atwood (1982) confronts that life of being writer and woman in "On Being a Woman Writer." Using her own word, I would characterize Atwood's writing as being filled with *tension.* Writing about the stereotypes heaped upon writers in general and women specifically, she explains, "The point about these stereotypes is that attention is focused not on the actual achievements of the authors, but on their lives, which are distorted and romanticized; their work is then interpreted in the light of the distorted version" (p. 200).

Her argument, a valid one, I believe, fills this discussion with tension. I hope to avoid reducing Atwood's writing to how it looks in terms of her life, but I also believe her life does matter. Another concern voiced by Atwood (1982) is the tendency readers, teachers, and critics have to associate writers with causes: "The two Messages I'm most frequently saddled with are Women's Lib and Canadian Nationalism, though I belong to no formal organization devoted to either" (p. 201). So as I discuss the patterns of Atwood's writing, I am not implying that she presents any distinct or rote ideological agenda in her work. I do feel that with any writer, we as readers, students, and teachers can benefit from anticipating patterns in a writer's work while simultaneously expecting the unexpected.

In her discussion of being a woman writer, Atwood (1982) begins by discounting the "the value of writers . . . becoming directly involved in political movements of any sort," because that involvement turns out to be no "good for the writer" (p. 190). Yet, we will find that Atwood's writing is often highly political in nature, in that she gives metaphorical flesh and blood and bones to the political nature of human endeavors (such as her speculative *The Handmaid's Tale*). In this essay, she also acknowledges that women writers of her generation cannot escape that they exist in a culture yet to rectify clearly the perception of a woman's proper place—such as "it was still assumed that a woman's place was in the home and nowhere else" (p. 191). The cultural and political reality, according to Atwood, includes that women are labeled—in a way that is distinct from any criticisms leveled at men who write—"selfish," "wicked," or "neurotic" if they pursued writing as a career (p. 191).

Written in 1976, Atwood's essay reveals a great deal about both the sexism of modern society and Atwood as a person and a writer. Atwood (1982) admits that "prejudice against women will affect you *as a writer* not directly but indirectly," detailing throughout the piece that woman are objectified sexually in ways men are not, for example (p. 194). But the larger pattern embodied in this essay is common in Atwood's work: the tension and even anger you read in her writer's voice go along with her ability to work within an ideology such as feminism while simultaneously *not* parroting any ideological party line. That tension is captured well toward the end of the essay: "The woman writer, then, exists in a society that . . . has little respect for writing as a profession, and not much respect for women either" (p. 204). Yet, this comment is no reason to fret or complain; for Atwood it means simply "[t]he proper path is to become better as a writer" (p. 204).

With Atwood's skepticism in mind, I would like to share the thematic patterns identified by Cooke (2004), patterns she effectively sees flowing into Atwood's work from her life. One theme running through Atwood's work is her "focus on ecological awareness," which "can be traced to her father and the lifestyle he established for his family" (Cooke, p. 3). Atwood's childhood brought her close to nature, Cooke explains, and from that concern for the ecology, Atwood also developed a sincere appreciation for the unity of all living creatures. Addressing ecological themes in her work is intertwined with Atwood's confronting "man's inhumanity to man," argues Cooke (p. 6).

A second theme, feminism, identified by Cooke (2004) can be linked to Atwood's mother, whose family "modeled possibilities for women beyond the roles generally available to women of Atwood's own generation" (pp. 6–7). I suggest that Atwood is better described as a writer compelled to dramatize the complex and contradictory nature of how the world treats women and how women function both as humans and as women, best captured in *The Handmaid's Tale*. Cooke concludes that "[t]his project of exposure has become a central tenet of all her writing—fiction, nonfiction, and poetry" (p. 9).

"[W]riting in, about, and on behalf of Canada" represents the third thematic element identified by Cooke (2004, p. 9). While I as a non-Canadian would add that we can read and embrace Atwood's work with little knowledge of Canada, I would also argue that the specific connection Cooke makes between Atwood and Canada is as important in many ways as acknowledging the importance of *place* in

Atwood's writing. Atwood's life and writing have both been grounded in the places of her living, and Canada has played a pivotal role in that without doubt.

While I cannot fully leave Atwood's life behind at any point in this book, I now turn to outlining as fully as possible her varied and impressive body of work. The chapter then ends with discussions of Atwood's position within literary traditions and her tools and techniques as a writer.

Works of Atwood

The importance of any artist is often linked to both the quantity and quality of his or her work. Atwood's works often receive popular and critical praise, and she offers her readers not only an impressive number of works but also an impressive span of genres. The following outline of most of her published works should provide readers, students, and teachers a useful storehouse of works to bring into the classroom.

Her first novel, *The Edible Woman* (1969), "provides a critique of North American consumer society in the 1960s from a woman's, and more specifically from a feminist, point of view" (Cooke, 2004, p. 31). Marian MacAlpin, the main character, loses her appetite throughout the novel, a social satire that would become a key element of many of Atwood's novels. Set in Toronto, the story revolves around Marian—her relationship with Peter, her roommate Ainsley, and her work in market research. In Chapter Three, I explore this novel more closely as one of the early novels we can bring into the classroom. *Surfacing* (1972), Atwood's second novel, is similar in theme and style to Atwood's poetry, argues Stein (1999). The unnamed protagonist is a woman returning to her childhood home, northern Quebec, and facing the disappearance of her father. Cooke (2004) compares this work to Jack Kerouac's *On the Road,* suggesting its themes deal with the journey and self-discovery; she adds that Atwood's work is distinct, however, because those themes are told "not only from the point of view of a woman, but also from the point of view of a *Canadian* woman" (p. 54). Along with self-discovery, the novel addresses several tensions—nationalism (Canadian and American), wilderness and urban life, relationships (family and romantic struggles between men and women). Atwood infuses the work with many mythic labels, a pattern we will explore more fully in Chapter Three.

Joan Foster, under the pseudonym Louisa K. Delcourt, is the author of Gothic romance novels and Atwood's narrator in *Lady Oracle* (1976). "The novel both parodies and exploits the features of

the Gothic tradition," explains Stein (1999), adding, "in the process raising questions about writing, identity, the distinctions between serious art and escape fiction, the author's control of her text, the place of the writer in society, the interconnections and confusions of literature and life, and the functions of literature" (p. 57). Ideal for the English classroom where we explore literature and writing, this novel is one of Atwood's humorous works that raises key social issues—again perfect for students in high school and college. Joan's life is offered in flashbacks, and the plot reveals her difficult past and watches her fake her death in order to seek a fresh beginning in Italy. This fantastic plot grows from the narrator's struggles with her fame as a writer and her relationships with men.

A finalist for the Governor General's Award (a prestigious Canadian literary award), *Life Before Man* (1979) is notable for containing Atwood's first male narrator and the rotating narration of three characters—Nate and Elizabeth Schoenhof (a married couple) along with Lesje Green (Nate's lover). While many readers and critics acknowledge the lack of action in the novel—also noted by one of the characters—the work does include romantic tension, attempted rape, suicide and attempted suicide, and death.

CONNECTIONS

Stein (1999) notes that Atwood has identified *Life Before Man* as a "homage to George Eliot's *Middlemarch*" (p. 66). A novel unit pairing these novels could explore their use of "'multiple discourses'" and their "argu[ments] against scientific determinism" (Stein, p. 66). While many note that few critics and teachers deal with *Life Before Man,* the novel contains similarities to *The Wizard of Oz,* providing another interesting connection for the classroom.

Called an "overtly political novel," *Bodily Harm* (1981) follows journalist Renata Wilford or "Rennie," as she flees to the Caribbean to work and recover from breast cancer (Stein, 1999, p. 71). In St. Antoine, she becomes romantically involved with Paul and the rising political unrest of the island. Critics note that Atwood implements the conventions of a detective thriller in this novel as part of her feminist theme. The novel addresses the politics of relationships between men and women as well as the larger political issues that often surface in Atwood's works, such as the violence and oppression suffered by women.

Winner of the 1987 Arthur C. Clarke Award, *The Handmaid's Tale* (1985) stands as Atwood's most acclaimed and most taught work— a dystopian novel that weaves a keen eye for both the historical errors of humanity and the failures we continue to practice. Set in bible-based Gilead, the work is highly structured in its narrative format as well as being intricately plotted and designed as a fictional world that is all too real. The main character, Offred/June, reveals the story through the transcript of an audio-taped narrative; much of this alternate world is revealed through that narrative, but the final section offers even more insight and satire through a scholarly conference exploring the now-defunct society. Chapter Four will explore this and other dystopian novels more closely.

Cat's Eye (1989) is one of Atwood's art novels, focusing on painter Elaine Risley and her memories of her childhood and teen years. Elaine returns to Toronto, and the novel explores her own struggles with her past and with her roles as an artist and a woman. Cooke (2004) explains that "[i]n the artist novels . . . , where women are cast in the role of artist rather than artist's model, we hear artists and storytellers reflect on their art" (p. 97). In this novel, Cooke adds, "The lesson for Atwood's readers is that we must pay close attention not only to what the artist says about her art but also to what the art itself can say and, perhaps more importantly, do" (p. 98). In Chapter Five, we will look more closely at this novel, notably the extensive use of allusions to Shakespeare's *Macbeth*.

In *The Robber Bride* (1993), three women—Roz, Charis, and Tony—reveal varying views of a woman who serves as their common rival, Zenia. Stein (1999) notes that "Atwood's novels frequently involve doubles and doubling; this novel has four central figures and plays multiple variations on its central themes" (p. 96). Atwood manipulates the Robber Bride folktale in order to deal with female-male relationships along with the nature of friendship. Stein adds that the novel, set in Toronto during the latter half of the twentieth century, "explores and problematizes questions of identity, good and evil, heterosexual relationships, friendship, war, history, and victimization, but above all of storytelling," making the work ideal for our classrooms (p. 96). This novel will be included in Chapter Five's discussion.

Alias Grace (1996), awarded the 1996 Giller prize, is "based on the story of Grace Marks, a housemaid accused of murdering her employer and his housekeeper in 1843. The novel combines social realism, comedy of manners, epistolary form, Gothic fiction, and even a ballad" (Stein, 1999, p. 103). The mid-nineteenth-century murder of Thomas Kinnear and Nancy Montgomery in Canada led to the hanging of James McDermott and the imprisonment of Grace Marks, who was released after nearly thirty years, moving to New York where she was lost to history. Atwood fictionalizes these historical events but focuses heavily on a central aspect of the murder and trial—the ambiguity concerning Marks' guilt and how the justice system deals differently with

men and women. Although this novel seems, at first blush, much different from Atwood's other novels, the narration soon reveals itself as very much her work: "*Murderer* is merely brutal. It's like a hammer, or lump of metal. I would rather be a murderess than a murderer, if those are the only choices" (*Alias Grace,* p. 23). I will also discuss this novel more fully in Chapter Five.

Atwood challenges the reader's perceptions and expectations of genre, villainy, gender roles in society, and gender within literature in *The Blind Assassin* (2000). This novel garnered the 2000 Booker Prize and the 2001 Hammett Prize, incorporating a story within a story in this ambitious work. The main character, Iris Chase, has lost her sister Laura to suicide soon after World War II; Iris recalls her long life, in her 80s during the present of the narration—including her marriage to Richard Griffen and her sister's novel (included in the narration and sharing the title of Atwood's novel). Cooke (2004) explains that "Iris is a wonderful example of how one character can be so steeped in the rank darkness of villainy and self-deception and still appear so beguilingly sympathetic" (p. 138).

At first *Oryx and Crake* (2003) appears to be quite similar to, being another dystopian novel, *The Handmaid's Tale.* In both novels, modern society has collapsed, but this more recent work leans more toward the post-Apocalyptic tradition, addressing the rise of a theocracy out of social upheaval. In *The Handmaid's Tale,* Atwood addresses the dangers of science as it mixes with human frailties, but in *Oryx and Crake,* her concern for technology and science in forms we all enjoy is expanded—as is her warning about the potential dangers in those advances. The narrative follows Snowman, who finds himself with his friend Crake and his love Oryx. These characters—marked by child pornography and biotechnology—are revealed more fully to the reader through flashbacks as Snowman wanders through the fractured remains of the world he has lost.

"A feminist perspective on Homer from Margaret Atwood? We're shocked," Hand (2005) offers, tongue in cheek, in her review of Atwood's *The Penelopiad* (2005). The story is classic Homer—Penelope explaining her wait for Odysseus and the complications of her life during those years. In her introduction to the work, Atwood argues, "The story as told in *The Odyssey* doesn't hold water: there are too many inconsistencies. I've always been haunted by the hanged maids; and, in *The Penelopiad,* so is Penelope herself" (p. xv). This narrative explores the nature of mythology and legend—since Atwood explains that she draws on more than the printed text of *The Odyssey* for her version of Penelope's plight—along with continuing her quest to unravel the mystery of being a woman in a man's world (even from the grave).

CONNECTIONS

Though obvious, *The Penelopiad* is an ideal pairing for *The Odyssey* and other tales of mythology. As I discuss later in this chapter, Atwood's work has a postmodern element in which she confronts classic expectations and patterns while simultaneously working within those expectations and patterns. In this work, she does just that with mythology and with narrative perspective. Many students may become more interested in mythology through a retelling such as this one. A companion pairing that might follow this one is John Gardner's *Grendel* and its source, *Beowulf*.

Atwood's fame among readers tends to be focused heavily on her novels, with some familiar with her impressive poetry and short fiction. Her nonfiction, however, is a wonderful source for our classrooms. Her book-length nonfiction collection includes the following titles: *Survival: A Thematic Guide to Canadian Literature* (1972), *Days of the Rebels 1815–1840* (1977), *Second Words: Selected Critical Prose* (1982), *Strange Things: The Malevolent North in Canadian Literature* (1995), *Two Solicitudes: Conversations [with Victor-Lévy Beaulieu]* (1998), *Negotiating with the Dead: A Writer on Writing* (2003), *Writing with Intent: Essays, Reviews, Personal Prose: 1982–2004* (2004/2005). The books here that I will discuss for classroom use are similar to the nonfiction collections of Kurt Vonnegut in that she collects a wide variety of nonfiction works that had been previously published.

Atwood offers our students wonderful personal essays, journalism, arguments, literary musings, reviews, speeches, lectures, criticism, political discussions, and more. Throughout, her gifts as a writer and as a thinker are as sharp and engaging as in her novels and poetry. "Inertia is my constant companion, procrastination my household pet. If I'm not eager and keen and resolved and strenuously bent, I find it very difficult to write at all," she writes in the introduction to *Writing with Intent* (p. xvii). It is that voice and that passion that will most engage our students as readers and ultimately as writers of nonfiction themselves. Chapter Two will look extensively at bringing her nonfiction into our classrooms as part of our reading and writing curriculums.

"Margaret Atwood's remarkable literary career encompasses all genres . . . ; however, it was her poetry that first built her reputation," explains Stein (1999, p. 9). Her published collections of poetry clearly rival her impressive list of novels—*The Circle Game* (1964), *The Animals in That Country* (1969), *The Journals of Susanna Moodie* (1970), *Procedures for Underground* (1970), *Power Politics* (1971), *You Are Happy* (1974),

Selected Poems (1976), *Two-Headed Poems* (1978), *True Stories* (1981), *Interlunar* (1984), *Selected Poems II: Poems Selected and New, 1976–1986* (1986), *Selected Poems 1966–1984* (1990), *Margaret Atwood Poems 1965–1975* (1991), *Morning in the Burned House* (1995), and *Eating Fire: Selected Poems, 1965–1995* (1998). Critics (Wilson, 2003) tend to discuss many thematic similarities between Atwood's poetry and fiction—along with noting similar evolutions in how she addresses those themes. Poems, like short stories and essays, are wonderful texts to bring into the classroom since they are brief; her poems provide fertile opportunities for pairing her poetry with a larger novel unit. Chapter Seven will discuss the matter of using Atwood's poetry in the classroom in greater detail.

Dancing Girls (1977), *Murder in the Dark* (1983), *Bluebeard's Egg* (1983), *Wilderness Tips* (1991), *Good Bones* (1992), *The Tent* (2006) and *Moral Disorder: And Other Stories* (2006) form a group of impressive collections of short fiction. "Atwood's stories combine realism and whimsy, fairy tale, myth, and fantasy as they represent the lives of contemporary women and men struggling to cope with an often puzzling or difficult world," according to Stein (1999, p. 125), who notes the essential concern in Atwood's short fiction for characters. One story, "Rape Fantasies," illustrates Atwood's ability to offer a compelling narrative through an engaging voice; the story reveals itself as an ambiguous discussion by the female character as shared with her date who appears to be—at least in her mind—a potential rapist. As with many of her short stories, this work addresses contemporary issues (date rape became an issue that frequently appeared on the cover of women's magazines in the 1970s and 1980s) through a narrative voice that leaves the reader uncomfortable both with the tone and the topic—Is some of this funny? Is the woman about to be raped? The full discussion of Atwood's short stories in the classroom will be in Chapter Six.

The brief outlines offered above cover the bulk of Atwood's work, but she also has published children's books, literary criticism, and her own artwork. I hope that this introduction to her works accomplishes two purposes—proving her distinction as a major writer in contemporary times and supporting my argument that she deserves to be brought into our classrooms in a wide array of genres. In her *Negotiating with the Dead,* Atwood (2002) reveals that she is keenly aware of the tension that exists among reader, writer, and text—an issue we wrestle with in our classrooms daily:

> Messengers always exist in a triangular situation—the one who sends the message, the message-bearer, whether human or inorganic, and the one who receives the message. Picture, therefore, a triangle, but not a complete triangle: something more like an upside-down V. (p. 125)

She continues by explaining that the communication between writer and reader is linked directly to the text. Her texts serve us well as we try to teach our students as young readers and young writers.

Themes, Tendencies, and Craft in a Writer's Writer

Reingard M. Nischik (2000) describes Atwood with high praise:

> A spokeswoman for human rights—of which her acute awareness of gender differences forms an integral part—a Canadian nationalist, a brilliant observer of contemporary Western culture who in her works questions conventional modes of perception and evaluation, Atwood is one of the most important literary chroniclers of our time. (p. 1)

Here, along with the endorsement for Atwood's gifts, is a critic attempting to capture the nature of a great and complex writer without oversimplifying those gifts. That is my challenge in the next paragraphs.

For young readers, distinguishing among the various qualities of writers is a real challenge. Popular and genre writers—often held in lower regard by the academic world—are not distinct from writers of serious fiction in the eyes of those young readers. When we discuss tendencies of serious literary writers (the type of writers we are likely to teach and value in classrooms), we must be cautious not to reduce those writers to one-trick ponies. In other words, if our students become aware that genre writers are often seen as beneath "serious" writers, we must be clear with those students how literary critics make those distinctions when the serious writers also produce work that could be called genre literature. If we do not make such a distinction, then students may see literary criticism as arbitrary judgments. Now, I want to offer some of the tendencies in themes, concerns, and technique often found in Atwood's works, noting that the quality of her writing is far more important than any labels we might assign any of her works., noting that she is typically a writer who defies generalizations. Let's begin to examine some of her omnipresent themes and topics.

Ecology. Cooke (2004) recognizes that Atwood's concern for the natural world—tenuous in the hands of humans—can be traced to her upbringing. Her poems, short stories, and novels throughout her career have consistently addressed the delicate balance of nature. *Wilderness Tips* (1991) is an obvious example. She appears to feel a need to raise her reader's awareness of each person's role in nature, of each person's place as one aspect of nature. Atwood may be distinctly

Canadian in regard to her childhood in the wilderness associated with Canada, but her ecological themes fit well into the U.S. literary tradition (Emerson and Thoreau) and the British tradition of valuing nature in the works of the Romantics, such as Wordsworth, Keats, and others.

Technology and Science. In a lecture, Atwood (1995) joked while discussing her genesis as a poet, "[T]he biologist in me became very interested in the different varieties of moulds that could be grown on a leftover Kraft dinner"—highlighting her scientific nature beneath her literary exterior. Her concern for the promises and dangers of technology and science parallels in many ways the concerns of Barbara Kingsolver (Thomas, 2005a) and Kurt Vonnegut (Thomas, 2006)—all three of whom share both a scientific nature and a strong skepticism concerning technology and science. Particularly central in her dystopian works, *The Handmaid's Tale* and *Oryx and Crake,* themes and plot elements connected with science and technology are essential aspects of Atwood's works.

Feminism. "[H]er mother's family modeled possibilities for women beyond the roles generally available to women of Atwood's own generation," explains Cooke (2004, p. 6), as noted above. This observation by Atwood's biographer provides a foundation for Atwood being "acutely aware of the double standards facing women and . . . [being] prepared to use her writing to expose them" (Cooke, p. 9). What feminism means in Atwood's writing is that she is keenly aware that gender does matter, that much of history and of the contemporary world revolves around the sex of any person—more often than not to the disadvantage of females. I would argue that Atwood, however, is not an ideologue for radical feminism although some may try to discount her as such, but her work reveals a writer exploring the ambiguity in issues of gender.

Canadian Nationalism. Most critics acknowledge that Atwood's international fame and acclaim have contributed positively to a view of Canadian literature as a distinct tradition; Atwood has written about and worked for the Canadian tradition as an advocate as well. Of course, Atwood's voice and persona are Canadian; further, much of her fiction is set in Canada. This tendency is pronounced, yet it seems that many readers can and often do feel drawn to her work without understanding fully or even recognizing the Canadian elements of her work. However, Cooke (2004) argues that "[a]nalyses of her work can be significantly enriched by attention to the Canadian literary and cultural context" (p. 24)—one additional way we can expand the patterns of our English classrooms.

Postmodernism. Briefly, we can characterize postmodern writers as those who confront assumptions about traditional thoughts and conventions. The postmodern writer sees a world of relative truth and revels in raising questions while often balking at offering definitive answers (since answers can often lead to dogma). Embedded in many of her other themes and topics is Atwood's tendency to question—the roles of men and women, the locus of power in society, the value of organized religion, humans' inhumanity to other humans, the value of capitalism, etc. Atwood's manipulation of writing forms and conventions also places her in a postmodern tradition. *Oryx and Crake* looks and reads as most novels do, but when a reader opens *Alias Grace,* within a few pages, he or she knows this is not a typical novel; reading *The Tent* leaves the reader equally disoriented about genre.

Visual Art and Writing. The main character of *Cat's Eye* is an artist; throughout Atwood's works, we find a genuine interest in and consideration of all sorts of artists—whether visual artists or writers. She has novels with a story-within-a-story—allowing her to muse through fiction about writing fiction. She directly addresses her primary art in nonfiction with *Negotiating with the Dead.* Her themes and topics both endorse the value of art for humanity and offer some insight into how artists function, how art is produced. That her fiction and nonfiction consider the act of being a writer is one of the best reasons to bring Atwood into our classrooms.

Social Commentary. Cooke (2004) feels that "Atwood's gift is that at the same time that her work challenges and disturbs, it also entertains. As its author, then, she is both literary celebrity and moral conscience" (p. 29). That moral conscience slices open our human weaknesses and social flaws. In *The Handmaid's Tale* she exposes the largest possible issues of human nature and social dynamics; in other works, her social commentary works at the lower levels of daily individual interactions. Regardless, as a postmodern artist, she is confronting the assumptions of government, family, religion, and all of our social constructs. Most of those confrontations seem to ask why we can't find humane practices as humans.

Relationships—Love, Friendship, Family. Many of our most often read and taught works of literature are essentially dramatizations of human interactions, human relationships. Whether romantic love or friendship or familial love, these relationships fascinate readers and writers alike. Atwood's works explore relationships, usually in terms of the female-male dynamic but also in terms of the complications that rise from any relationship. *Cat's Eye* stands as a solid example of Atwood's gift for creating complex and dynamic relationships that engage and disorient the reader; in this novel, she looks closely at women's friendships—uncovering the darkness of those relationships. What often distinguishes Atwood's look at relationships is her tendency to manipulate the readers' expectations and assumptions about both relationships and literary depictions of relationships.

Politics. When asked about her politics and writing, Atwood responded, "People talking about politics usually start from the ass end backwards in that they think you have a political agenda, and then you make your work fit that cookie cutter. It's the other way around" (Snell, 1997)—acknowledging that her work *is* political, though probably not in the way most people believe. In the same interview, Atwood adds, "As an artist your first loyalty is to your art." While we can safely argue that much of Atwood's work is political, we should be clear that artists who consider their work "high art" or "serious art" are driven primarily as artists. When any work slips toward having a political agenda, when the artist becomes an ideologue, then we no longer have art—Atwood and others would argue. If we look closely at one of her most overtly political works, *The Handmaid's Tale,* we can see that Atwood is most concerned with how political dynamics tend historically to work against the dignity and freedom of humans, in a tradition we might associate with George Orwell.

Alienation. Snowman in *Oryx and Crake,* Offred/June in *The Handmaid's Tale,* Grace Marks in *Alias Grace*—these, just to mention a few, are characters profoundly alienated, though in nuanced and different ways. Writers often acknowledge alienation in their works, a major and persistent theme in art. I believe Atwood addresses two aspects of alienation. She dramatizes the many conditions that contribute to a human *being* alienated and *feeling* alienated. The second—and often for me the more interesting—aspect is that she captures and expresses how characters *feel* when alienated. Some of the most haunting passages of *The Handmaid's Tale* are Offred/June's moments when she realizes she is not only alone—without her husband and child—but also losing even the memory of the ones she loves.

History. "When I was young I believed that 'nonfiction' meant 'true.' But you read a history written in, say, 1920 and a history of the same events written in 1995 and they're very different. There may not be one Truth—there may be several truths—but saying that is not to say that reality doesn't exist," Atwood shows here her keen perception of perspective in history (Snell, 1997). In her nonfiction, poetry, and fiction, Atwood reveals her own complex and extensive historical knowledge and understanding. Atwood titles the last section of her most famous novel, *The Handmaid's Tale,* "Historical Notes," where she presents a fictional academic conference in order to share with her readers the wealth of history she weaves into her dystopian work. *Alias Grace,* of course, grows entirely from an actual sensational murder and trial in Canada.

Academia. As mentioned above, the last section of *The Handmaid's Tale* provides Atwood an opportunity to satirize the academic world—a world with which she has had an ambiguous relationship. Her biography shows that her life as a learner broadly and as a student specifically was a major aspect of the artist she has become, but her academic pursuit ended just short of a doctorate. She has written often about her less than fulfilling experiences at Harvard, where she faced sexism and came to terms with the disappointing qualities of higher education. When she deals with academia, Atwood tends to offer a heavy dose of satire—often blending in how academia still suffers from sexist patterns and the unfair weight of whose voice matters.

Duplicity. "I collect con-artist stories. One of my favorites is that of a Portuguese woman who had been passing herself off not only as a man but in the military establishment as a general," Atwood shared in an interview (Snell, 1997). Critics note that many of Atwood's stories revolve around duplicity, tricksters drawn from legends and mythology. This theme or pattern appears to fit well with her concerns about the treatment of women in society as well as the devices women have used in order to overcome oppressive elements of many different societies.

Empowerment and Victimization. Atwood's works explore, without doubt, people (often women) who are victims of some degree of oppressions, yet, Atwood (Snell, 1997) herself sees the circumstances of empowerment and victimization differently than these terms might mean to most:

Let us change it from victimhood to people in circumstances that put some pressure on them, which is not quite the same thing. Some people tell me that Grace Marks is a victim and I say, "Hey, just hang on a minute.

What about Nancy and Thomas? They're the ones who ended up dead in the cellar." I don't think it's quite as simple as "These people over here are always the oppressors, and these people over here are always victims."

Her reference to *Alias Grace* can just as easily be applied to many of her works, such as Offred in *The Handmaid's Tale.*

Human Rights. More universal than her social commentary is Atwood's quest as an artist for human rights—a quest that also adds nuance and complexity to her other tendencies such as feminism. Many artists are driven by the human condition, and Atwood writes often in a variety of genres what could be characterized as arguments for *improving* the conditions of every human. If we recall her comments about being political in her art, however, we should be clear that these arguments are artistic and not dogmatic.

Few who treasure Atwood's novels know Atwood the cartoonist, the visual artist, but Atwood is truly an *artist.* Her primary tools for her art, however, are words and sentences. The craft of writing is as compelling in her writing as her ideas, her characters, and her narratives. Just as she has patterns to her themes and topics, Atwood reveals patterns in her tools as a writer, a wordsmith; some of the dominant techniques and elements in her works include the following:

- *Gothic elements—darkness.* Cooke (2004) writes extensively in her consideration of Atwood about the dominant gothic elements in Atwood's work—"its fascination with ambiguous characterization, eerie settings, and the evocation of terror, to cite the key characteristics of the gothic aesthetic" (p. 11). Cooke continues by detailing four different levels of darkness in Atwood, since the quality is central to Atwood's work.
- *Color imagery.* While reading and studying *The Handmaid's Tale,* a former student of mine noticed that the hotel room colors are complimentary colors; the student was an art student and had learned about complimentary colors in her art class. Color—purposeful color—weaves its way through much of Atwood's writing, drawing her work as a writer and visual artist together.
- *Narrative voice, persona.* Howells (1995) recognizes that "as a 'true novelist' [Atwood] is interested in the dynamic powers of language and story"; thus, her work is characterized by powerful narrative voices (p. 19). Narration and voice are often difficult techniques for student writers to master. In Atwood, students find a powerful example of *control* in her use of narration and voice. In her poetry, she creates similarly powerful personas.
- *Genre, conventions.* As a scholar and an artist, Atwood is both keenly aware of and highly skeptical of the conventions of genre. Her writing, then, incorporates and manipulates those conventions of genre (often leaving the reader somewhat disoriented, often pre-

senting writing that is difficult to categorize clearly) as a technique for creating her themes, her implications—many of which are designed to challenge conventional structures as well as conventional thought.

- *Setting, place.* "This sense of location is the basis of Atwood's realism," explains Howells (1995, p. 11), noting Atwood's use of her homeland, Canada. The details of setting are vibrant and engaging in her work, but Atwood also indicates through those details that this existence is always bound by place (and ultimately by time also).

- *Characterization.* Inexperienced readers are often drawn disproportionately to the importance of plot; this is even more pronounced among novice writers. Yet, our best writers value characters above all else. Atwood's fiction lives because of the people she creates; those characters span a wide spectrum of types—although they all are fascinating.

- *Satire, parody.* Part of Atwood's darkness grows from her tendency toward satire, her biting humor with a serious intent. Atwood can be simply funny, but much of her satire is dark, eliciting more thought and discomfort than laughter.

- *Archetypal (mythological) patterns.* The bones of Atwood's stories are the patterns of fables, legends, and myth. The tension in her work often grows from Atwood's manipulation of these archetypal patterns. Atwood appears to be interested in both the universal and the unique, the classic and the contemporary, drawing them together in her use of myth.

In *The Tent,* Atwood (2006) speaks of the young:

> I have decided to encourage the young. Once I wouldn't have done this, but now I have nothing to lose. The young are not my rivals. Fish are not the rivals of stone. (p. 17)

And I hope this introductory chapter encourages old and young alike to read, learn, and teach the works of Atwood. Chapter Two looks at her nonfiction as a way to expand the canon of our reading lists and as models for students as writers themselves.

FOR FURTHER STUDY-MARGARET ATWOOD

Books

Cooke, N. (1998). *Margaret Atwood: A biography.* Toronto: ECW Press.
Cooke acknowledges that this is not an authorized biography, adding that Atwood did cooperate to some degree with Cooke during the project. Early

in the work, Cooke notes that "[Atwood believes] that the artist is a responsible citizen and not a passive victim" (p. 17). The biography reveals just such a woman and writer as artist. While this biography is becoming somewhat dated, it is an excellent introduction to Atwood's life, suitable for both teachers and students.

Cooke, N. (2004). *Margaret Atwood: A critical companion.* Westport, CT: Greenwood Press.

Cooke offers a very effective and accessible critical look at Atwood within a series from Greenwood Press that is also excellent for teachers and students. This critical volume is more recent than Cooke's biography of Atwood though the two works do share some similarities. Here, Cooke begins with a brief biography, followed by placing Atwood within literary traditions. Chapters Three through Eight explore individual novels—*The Edible Woman, Surfacing, Lady Oracle, Cat's Eye, The Handmaid's Tale,* and *The Blind Assassin.* The only weakness in this volume is that is deals exclusively with novels, ignoring Atwood's wide range of publications in a variety of genres.

Howells, C. A. (1995). *Modern novelists: Margaret Atwood.* New York: St. Martin's Press.

Howells begins with a general chapter about Atwood and then addresses several of Atwood's major works—*Surfacing, Survival, Wilderness Tips, The Edible Woman, Lady Oracle, The Robber Bride, Life Before Man, Bodily Harm, The Handmaid's Tale,* and *Cat's Eye.* In Chapter One, Howells makes an excellent overall comment: "In Atwood's fiction there are no essentialist definitions of 'woman' or 'feminism' or even 'Canadian,' but instead representations of the endless complexity and quirkiness of human behavior which exceeds ideological labels and the explanatory power of theory" (p. 19).

Nischik, R. M., ed (2000). *Margaret Atwood: Works and impact.* Rochester, NY: Camden House.

This extensive volume includes four sections of essays by noted critics of Atwood—Life and Status, Works, Approaches, and Creativity—Transmission—Reception. Nischik includes photographs of Atwood and cartoons by Atwood. The bibliography of books by and on Atwood is also very helpful, though a bit dated. In the introduction, Nischik notes that this comprehensive and introductory collection "was prepared for the occasion of Margaret Atwood's sixtieth birthday" (p. 1).

Rigney, B. H. (1978). *Madness and sexual politics in the feminist novels: Studies in Bronte, Woolf, Lessing, and Atwood.* Madison: The University of Wisconsin Press.

Rigney explains in her introduction that this volume "attempts to reconcile feminism and psychology in the area of literary criticism" through four major feminist authors (p. 3). For our purposes here, the introduction frames critical approaches to feminist literature, a framework we should understand and share with students. Further, Chapter Four explores Atwood's *Surfacing* within that context. Rigney ends her chapter on *Surfacing:* "To the protagonist belongs the ultimate sanity: the knowledge that woman can descend, and return—sane, whole, victorious" (p. 115). The brief final chapter pulls all four authors and Rigney's previous discussions together; the book could provide a basis for a four-novel unit—*Jane Eyre, Mrs. Dalloway, The Four-Gated City,* and *Surfacing*—as well.

Stein, K. F. (1999). *Margaret Atwood revisited.* New York: Twayne Publishers.

Stein's work on Atwood is included in the Twayne's World Authors Series, one of many series by this publisher that is accessible to both teachers and students. Stein divides her book into eight chapters that cover Atwood's poetry, novels, short fiction, and a range of other works in a variety of genres. In the preface, Stein acknowledges Atwood's gifts as a storyteller as well as her concerns for social and political themes, adding: "Her texts question social, political, and literary ideas, beliefs, and conventions as they delight, inform, intrigue, and sometimes irritate" (p. xi).

VanSpanckeren, K., & Castro, J. G., eds. (1988). *Margaret Atwood: Vision and forms.* Carbondale: Southern Illinois University Press.

VanSpanckeren, in the introduction, explains that this collection of essays on Atwood's works (including a brief autobiographical essay by Atwood herself) is "for them [U.S. students and citizens], and the concerned reader" who "need . . . to enlarge their acquaintance with international affairs and assume the responsibility that comes with power" (p. xxvii). While some aspects of this collection are dated, the book includes a good collection of color reproductions of Atwood's watercolors.

Wilson, S. R., ed. (2003). *Margaret Atwood's textual assassinations: Recent poetry and fiction.* Columbus: The Ohio State University Press.

Sharon R. Wilson collects ten essays addressing Atwood's work in the 1980s and 1990s, notably her "ignored" writing and artwork characterized here as "assassinations" (p. xii). Major Atwood scholars discuss *Murder in the Dark, Good Bones and Simple Murders, Interlunar, Cat's Eye, Wilderness Tips, The Robber Bride, Morning in the Burned House, Alias Grace,* and *The Blind Assassin.* Wilson notes in the introduction: "In this book, we see how Margaret Atwood's recent texts not only continue genres and themes evident in her earliest work, but also intertextually advance innovative, genre-bending variations on these patterns" (p. xv).

Wilson, S. R., Friedman, T. B., & Hengen, S. (1996). *Approaches to teaching Atwood's* The Handmaid's Tale *and other works.* New York: The Modern Language Association of America.

Possibly the most often read, taught, and discussed work by Atwood is *The Handmaid's Tale.* The editors divide this practical work into two parts—Materials and Approaches. This book offers a wealth of information and support for teachers at many levels, from secondary classes through graduate coursework, and in a wide range of content areas—not just English or literature. Although primarily focused on *The Handmaid's Tale,* this book includes a great deal of information on many of Atwood's works.

Websites

O.W. Toad—Margaret Atwood Official Website (n.d.), http://www.owtoad.com.

This comprehensive official website has a quirky design that reflects Atwood's own unique nature. Once you click on the winged toad labeled "Enter," you find links as follows:

- What is new?—This link includes Upcoming Events by year and a What's New listing as well.
- From the Desk of Margaret Atwood—This link offers a wooden desk image that includes a variety of links (found in the six drawers of the desk)—Sound Clips (Poetry Readings), A Recent Poem, Worst Reviews Ever, Photo Album, Comics, and Book Covers.
- Table of Contents—This seems to be the main link, which includes a number of links—What's New, From the Desk of Margaret Atwood, Life and Time, On Writing, Book by Margaret Atwood, Books about Margaret Atwood, More Books about Margaret Atwood, Frequently Asked Questions, and Links to Other Sites.
- Go to the Links—Here, the site offers additional links related to Atwood, her publishers, Canadian literature, and other writers.
- Search—The site also has a search feature.

The Margaret Atwood Society (n.d.), http://www.mscd.edu/~atwoodso/index.htm.

The website opens with this statement that captures the society and site well:

> Welcome to the website of the Margaret Atwood Society, an international association of scholars, teachers and students who share an interest in Atwood's work. The main goal of the Society is to promote scholarly exchange of the writer's work by providing opportunities for scholars to exchange information.

The site includes several links—Home, About the Society, Officers, Calls for Papers, Conference Panels, Awards, and Links.

Margaret Atwood, *Oryx and Crake* (n.d.), http://www.oryxandcrake.co.uk.

This stylish site dedicated primarily to Atwood's *Oryx and Crake* opens with a gridded picture of a half-face of a young male and a half-face of a young female with the question, Do you believe in Crake?, in between. The links under "MARGARET ATWOOD" include Biography, Events, Interview, Q&A, Other Titled, Related Links, Contacts, and O.W. Toad. The links under "ORYX AND CRAKE" include Perfect Storm, Excerpt, Reading Guide, Further Reading, E-cards, Reviews, and Buy the Book.

Study Guide to Margaret Atwood: *The Handmaid's Tale,* Brians, P. (1995), Revised September 24, 2004, http://www.wsu.edu:8000/~brians/science_fiction/handmaid.html.

As the site title suggests, this is a study guide for Atwood's most-read work. The site has brief chapter-by-chapter explanations punctuated with thoughtful questions.

ENTRY POINTS AND CONNECTIONS

Middlemarch, George Eliot

The Wizard of Oz

The Odyssey, Homer

Grendel, John Gardner

Beowulf

Atwood's Intentional (Nonfiction) Writing

In her introduction to *Second Words: Selected Critical Prose,* Atwood (1982) reveals not only her own perceptions of nonfiction, but also the stigma cast over nonfiction by schooling; here, she explains her feelings about writing reviews, critical essays, and speeches:

> The real truth is that I don't like writing the kinds of things that are brought together in this volume nearly as much as I like writing other kinds of things. It's all too much like homework, which I never used to get done on time either, being, as most poets and novelists are, much fonder of looking out the window. (p. 11)

Later in the introduction when she asks, "Why do I find it so painful?" (p. 12), I am inclined to answer that the pain has been cultivated by the sparse experience students have with reading nonfiction and writing nonfiction in authentic circumstances and *by choice*—an argument I have made often. Here in Chapter Two, I want to discuss how we can bring Atwood's nonfiction into our classrooms in order to create those authentic experiences, thus avoiding our students feeling the same pain as Atwood does when they write nonfiction.

In this chapter, I focus on three collections of nonfiction by Atwood that are well suited to our English classes—*Second Words, Negotiating with the Dead,* and *Writing with Intent*—and touch on briefly a collection of interviews with Atwood published in 1990, *Margaret Atwood: Conversations.* I consider using Atwood's nonfiction as one way to expand the canon of our reading lists along with offering her nonfiction as models for students as writers. Let's look first at eight pieces in *Second Words* as avenues for exploring women writers (Adrienne Rich, Marge Piercy, Anne Sexton, and Sylvia Plath) and Atwood's early discussions of being a woman writer.

Women Writers—Of Curses and Selfishness

In *Second Words,* a great deal is revealed in Atwood's essay titles dealing with women as writers—"On Being a 'Woman Writer': Paradoxes and Dilemmas" and "The Curse of Eve—Or, What I Learned in School." The negative diction—we'll look closely at "paradoxes" and "curse" in this discussion—about the nature of being both woman and writer establishes the dilemma both for Atwood as a woman writer, but it also suggests a dilemma for all of us who teach the works of women writers, just as the passage at the opening of this chapter suggests, the role of school cannot be ignored when we consider our expectations and assumptions about women as writers.

If Atwood's implications about schooling are correct—the negative impact it has on our attitudes toward nonfiction *and* women writers—then we as teachers and students could benefit greatly from creating a matrix of our experiences and attitudes about each of these areas in order to facilitate an introductory discussion for this unit. While I feel that this should be done individually by each student, a matrix could also be completed in small groups; some prompting questions for this survey could include:

- Which women writers have you read, either in school or by choice? Do you have a favorite writer who is a woman? Why is she a favorite? A favorite work by a woman? Why?
- Who are the most memorable female characters about whom you have read (fiction)? Why are those female characters memorable?
- How do you define and distinguish between fiction and nonfiction? How do you feel about each? Do you prefer one instead of the other? Why?
- How much nonfiction have you read? Any favorite nonfiction? Why?
- Many of the writing assignments you have received in school have been nonfiction essays; how do you feel about writing nonfiction? What kinds of nonfiction have you written?

Regardless of how you phrase the prompting questions, this unit works best if you establish with students how they *feel* about women writers, women characters, and nonfiction (both their *reading* and *writing* nonfiction). After those feelings are established, as a class you can all consider how the feelings manifested themselves as well as how conceptions and assumptions about those issues can be changed through this unit of study.

After exploring their assumptions and expectations about women writers, female characters, and nonfiction, students can read either or both of the essays noted above—"On Being a 'Woman Writer,'" "The Curse of Eve"—in order to confront and reconsider those assumptions and expectations before moving on to Atwood's essays on and works by Adrienne Rich, Marge Piercy, Anne Sexton, and Sylvia Plath, when they can begin to experiment with their new vision of works by and about women (along with their own nonfiction writing).

"On Being a 'Woman Writer'" raises many nuanced concerns about attitudes toward women writers and female characters; the essay was written in 1976, providing an excellent opportunity for students to place her comments in historical context while debating how relevant her characterizations are for their generation. This essay is diligently crafted, thus serving as a model for students to write nonfiction creatively and purposefully themselves. The subtitle of the piece focuses Atwood's concerns on paradoxes and dilemmas, providing a sophisticated debate for the classroom. Here are some ideas confronted by Atwood in the essay:

- Atwood questions the "value of writers, male or female, becoming directly involved in political movements of any sort" (p. 190). The tension between being political and artistic is raised often by Atwood; here she places that tension within the larger issue of gender. Students can be prompted to discuss the political issue as well as how this plays out similarly or differently between men and women writers.

- Early in the essay, Atwood acknowledges the woman-as-housewife paradigm that has historically framed all women, including women who are drawn to art; this will be a key issue when students read the works of Rich, Piercy, Sexton, and Plath. Within this paradigm, Atwood notes, women who pursue their art have often confronted incredible guilt, forcing them to hide their work as artists—consider that Barbara Kingsolver wrote her first novel in a closet (Thomas, 2005a).

- One element that runs throughout Atwood's work is her ambiguous voice as a feminist; in this essay, she challenges feminist criticism, or at least the possible danger in such criticism: She "fear[s] . . . the development of a one-dimensional Feminist Criticism, a way of approaching literature produced by women that would award points according to conformity or nonconformity to an ideological position" (p. 192). This passage can be a wonderful entry point for discussions of both literary criticism (a spectrum of lenses) and the dangers of ideological stances (also lending itself to a consideration of inductive and deductive reasoning).

- While writing a biography of English educator Lou LaBrant for my dissertation, I was struck by LaBrant's persistent refusal to acknowledge *any* disadvantage for her being a woman in a man's world (Thomas, 2001). Atwood characterizes this phenomenon: "Such a woman tends to regard herself . . . as a sort of honorary man" (p. 193). This paradox confronts that some women *are* successful simultaneously with a great many women who have oppressed existences.

- Placing women as writers within a larger context of jobs traditionally considered women's professions, Atwood discusses the nature of being a writer: "[W]riting as a physical activity is private. You do it by yourself, on your own time," adding, "If you are a writer, prejudice against women will affect you *as a writer* not directly but indirectly" (pp. 193, 194).

- Later, she emphasizes the paradox again: "Woman and Writer are separate categories; but in any individual woman writer, they are inseparable" (p. 195). This comment and the ones offered above can be the basis for discussing both the roles of writers and the circumstances of women *as writers.*

- Most of us have heard the condescending "He throws like a girl" or the seemingly complimentary "She throws like a man." Atwood discusses the same dynamic in the art world: "This is a pattern in which good equals male, and bad equals female" (p. 197). Beyond this being a provocative and relevant point of debate for students, when students read and discuss Anne Sexton and Sylvia Plath, specifically, they should consider the tenuous reputation that these two poets embody since many critics see them as "Confessional Poets"—a label that is often belittling and grounded in assumptions concerning what counts as high art (characteristics drawn exclusively *by* men form the work *of* men).

- Since the mid-twentieth century, students have been educated in the analysis of literature by New Criticism standards that focus primarily on the text, excluding aspects of analysis such as the historical context of the author (or the plot) and the biography of the writer. The value in considering the biography of a writer when interpreting text is still highly debatable. Atwood wades into this debate: "The point about these stereotypes is that attention is focused not on the actual achievements of the authors, but on their lives, which are distorted and romanticized; their works are then interpreted in the light of the distorted version" (p. 200). Atwood offers a more complex view of the debate about interpreting text. It isn't the value of biography in those interpretations that concerns Atwood as much as her realization that biography is often a *distortion*. She is keenly aware of the stereotypes placed on both artists in general and women/women artists specifically. This passage may be a great opportunity to allow students to face their own stereotypes about artists and women artists (and to trace how those stereotypes have manifested themselves).

- The essay ends with a personal statement on being a writer, on being a woman writer. Part of that statement can serve as a writing prompt for students to reflect on the big issues of Atwood's piece: "The woman writer, then, exists in a society that, though it may turn certain individual writers into revered cult objects, has little respect for writing as a profession, and not much respect for women either" (p. 204).

While this essay raises important issues relevant to and needed by high school and college English students, some of Atwood's language is blunt so I recommend that any teacher read this carefully before sharing it with high school students.

As a transition to a unit on women writers—including Adrienne Rich, Marge Piercy, Anne Sexton, and Sylvia Plath—students should read "The Curse of Eve," a speech from 1978; it is a well-crafted piece that challenges the reader with a shifting and biting tone. This essay continues Atwood's consideration of women writers and female characters; it forces us as teachers and our students to look closely at how the academic world impacts those attitudes about women, writers, and writing (notably genre). After her initial comments identify the essentially sexist qualities she had found in the academic world, she states, "I escaped from academia and bypassed journalism" on her road to being "a professional writer" (p. 216). As she does in many pieces, Atwood establishes *formal* education as antithetical to being a writer.

One of the strongest aspects of the essay (in terms of it being ideal for the classroom) is Atwood's extended listing of female character types. This listing includes classic fairy tales and literature, but also includes comic super heroes, providing an opportunity to discuss the nature of archetypal patterns in many levels of art. Atwood acknowledges in this listing the worst aspects of these stereotypes and exposes students to a complex list that could ironically raise their thinking above those stereotypes. Her commentary with this list impacts students as readers and writers; too, it returns to her discussion of how the lives of women writers are often portrayed, distorted. One of her commentaries focuses on the stereotypical view of female poets, as insane, as recluses, as frail—regardless, Atwood argues for seeing the whole person who happens to be writer or the whole character who happens to be female: "[P]erhaps it is time to take the capital W off Woman" (Atwood, 1982, p. 227).

- -

CONNECTIONS

As a biographer, I became more and more convinced that students need some insight into the lives of writers. In the past several decades, more and more works are exploring the nature of biographies of women as new biographies are being written to re-examine the lives of women writers. For students and teachers, I recommend two works connected with these concepts raised by Atwood— *The Passion of Emily Dickinson,* Judith Farr (1992), and *Telling Women's Lives: The New Biography,* Linda Wagner-Martin (1994). I noticed that my ability to teach the works of Dickinson improved dramatically after I set aside the stereotypes I had mis-learned about her life (in school, of course) and began to explore her life with my students in ways prompted by Farr and Wagner-Martin—who also offers a very accessible biography on Sylvia Plath, *Sylvia Plath: A Biography* (1988).

- -

A second purpose for bringing this essay into the classroom is its use as a transition into studying the women writers Atwood reviews in *Second Words.* In "The Curse of Eve," Atwood mentions Plath and Sexton, adding, "Female writers in the twentieth century are seen not just as eccentric and unfeminine, but as doomed" (p. 226). She also notes that "[w]omen are still expected to be better than men"—to which she offers a "plea; women, both as characters and as people, must be allowed their imperfections" (pp. 226, 227). Atwood offers students (and their teachers) an opportunity to explore the works of women with a new lens, striving to avoid the assumptions that many have *learned:* "Even I may judge women more harshly than I do men; after all, they were responsible for Original Sin, or that is what I learned in school" (p. 228).

Using these first two essays and her reviews in *Second Words,* I recommend moving students into a unit on women writers that includes two writers who are fairly new to the canon, writers whose lives are often distorted in ways similar to Atwood's warning about biography—Anne Sexton and Sylvia Plath—and two writers who are too often unknown by students, writers who have complex and provocative life stories themselves—Marge Piercy and Adrienne Rich.

Atwood's "Anne Sexton: A Self-Portrait in Letters" begins with, "Anne Sexton was one of the most important American poets of her generation. She was both praised and condemned by critics for the intense 'confessional' quality of her poetry" (p. 287). Joined by time and their suicides, Sexton and Plath share a number of elements to their lives, their writing, and their reputations that are valuable for classroom considerations. In Atwood's brief review, students can find a wealth of information useful for studying Sexton's letters and her poetry—as well as her biography. Two of the gifts of Sexton's writing, whether her letters or her poetry, are her voice and her perspective—those confessional elements at the root of her ambiguous reputation as a valued writer. Toward the end of the review, Atwood offers a well-crafted and haunting point that serves the reader well when approaching Sexton—and many writers:

> A suicide is both a rebuke to the living and a puzzle that defies them to solve it. Like a poem, suicide is finished and refuses to answer questions as to its final cause. The unfortunate effect of such acts is to obscure the lives of their authors, leaving only the riddle of their deaths. (p. 289)

Atwood's review of Sylvia Plath's posthumous prose work, characterized as "a minor work by a major writer," is actually perfect in its brevity and its internal debate as an introduction to any works by Plath (p. 316). In this review, Atwood acknowledges the value of the reviewed work by Plath for the student, for those who wish to look deeply at the work of a writer whose reputation is still evolving (in some ways very similar to the evolving view of Sexton's work, though most place Plath ahead of Sexton). Here, Atwood discusses her own fascination with Plath's struggles as a writer in terms of the type of writer Plath longed to be. That struggle raises for students the debate over the quality of writing. Plath appears to have been drawn to the mass market (more money, less prestige) but has gradually achieved a literary reputation through her poetry. Atwood places Plath's initial ambitions as a writer in the context of Plath's marriage to a well-established poet, Ted Hughes—their relationship has been the basis of immense debate for decades.

About Marge Piercy, Atwood writes, "She is a serious writer who deserves the sort of considered attention which, too often, she does not get" (p. 272)—a sentiment that could be expressed about many women writers including the two above and Adrienne Rich. Atwood's discussion of *Woman on the Edge of Time* explains that many have failed to see the novel as a utopia, a form she admits attracts her (a good connection here if we are having students read *The Handmaid's Tale* or *Oryx and Crake*). This review becomes an argument for the fiction and poetry of Piercy, whose works are disturbing and engaging.

Since Piercy is rarely assigned and taught in schools, students might begin with her webpage (www.margepiercy.com) and build their view of her and her work with Atwood's cautions in mind.

Many similarities and some nuanced differences characterize the works of Adrienne Rich being added to our classrooms; she is a gifted writer who is best known as a poet but offers brilliant nonfiction as well. Three reviews of Rich's works are included in *Second Words*—"Adrienne Rich: *Diving into the Wreck*," "Adrienne Rich: *Poems, Selected and New*," and "Adrienne Rich: *Of Woman Born*." In *Diving into the Wreck,* the collection from which Rich's most anthologized poems come, Atwood notes the mythological reconsiderations running through the book: "The wreck she is diving into, in the very strong title poem, is the wreck of obsolete myths, particularly myths about men and women" (pp. 160–161). This comment reveals why Atwood is drawn to Rich and why Rich's work fits well into our English classes. Her second review of *Poems, Selected and New* serves as an argument for the value of Rich for poetry readers and writers, again endorsing Rich as suitable for the classroom. However, the third review in Atwood's collection stresses the importance of Rich as a writer of nonfiction. Throughout the three reviews, issues of Rich's feminism and her overtly political nature are raised, fitting well into Atwood's discussion of these issues in her own essays.

Atwood's *Second Words* includes many other valuable and teachable essays, but the unit suggested above can serve as a starting point for many discussions and writing opportunities for students who need to consider and reconsider issues of gender in society, issues of gender in writing and literature, and issues of genre—all exposed masterfully in this early collection. Next, we will turn to a more recent collection, *Negotiating with the Dead,* which is ideally suited for our English classes as writing workshops.

Atwood Writing for Writers

Atwood (2002) writes as a writer *to* writers in her *Negotiating with the Dead: A Writer on Writing.* Throughout this nonfiction book, she describes and analyzes her own evolution as a writer, from childhood until the present. Her Canadian education was British and "premodern," she explains, adding:

> Teaching focused on the texts, and the texts alone. We learned to memorize these texts, analyze their structure and style, and make précis of them, but none of them were placed in historical or biographical context. I suppose this was the spillover from the New Criticism, though nobody mentioned that term; and nobody talked about writing as a process or a profession—as something real people actually did. (pp. 13–14)

My experience has been, when reading about the lives of writers, that *how* writers become writers is more puzzling than logical—given the conditions of their schooling and sometimes their lives. The education Atwood received as a reader and writer was clearly dysfunctional in many respects; as teachers of English, we know that conditions in today's classrooms are different on the surface from hers, but I would argue that reading and writing instruction is often just as dysfunctional.

CONNECTION

How do writers, scholars, and artists become the people that they are? One way to uncover the evolution of a writer is to read biographies and memoirs. One brilliant memoir that addresses that evolution and how that looked in a woman's life is the wonderful and engaging *Vertigo* by Louise DeSalvo (1996), a Virginia Woolf scholar. Many of her reminiscences highlight moments in her young life as a student when she found moments with caring and insightful teachers who directly and indirectly fostered the scholar and writer (and reader) that she is. Students and teachers alike will value this book as a memoir and as a crafted piece of writing. Brief passages from this book-length work are also ideal for writing mini-lessons in our classrooms.

Before looking at how we can use *Negotiating with the Dead* in our English classes, primarily within our writing curriculum, let's clarify the conditions of many English classrooms in contemporary education (while these characteristics are primarily K-12 education, our college students have emerged out of these conditions). Jaeger (2006) captures well the state of reading instruction—scripted programs directly and indirectly mandated by U.S. federal legislation. The result is that students are forced to *cover* reading instruction quickly and that teachers are demoralized:

> Nevertheless, a clear message has been sent to any teacher in our district who might contemplate taking a stand that might be unpopular with administration: Speak up and you will be punished; advocate for your students and you will be silenced. (p. 41)

The state of reading instruction is far from authentic, resulting in students and teachers who are *less* empowered from that instruction, who are silenced.

Writing instruction has historically languished beneath math and reading in its importance since it has been less often tested and measured, yet, times have changed, and for the worst. Wilson (2006) has recently highlighted the increasingly negative impact that testing, rubrics, and computerized scoring of student writing have had on how we *teach,* how we *assess,* and how we *perceive* writing and the qualities of exceptional writing. Wilson subjected "My Name," by Sandra Cisneros, to a private company's computerized software to score student writing; the result, as we might guess, was that Cisneros's work was found to be quite flawed. Wilson also "corrected" Cisneros's piece, guided by the program's suggestions:

> But [the computer program] cannot recognize what writers do well. It only defines and describes deficits, and its feedback to Cisneros merely pointed out "mistakes" in "My Name"—repetitious word use, use of fragments, and problems with organization and development. (p. 45)

The current state of writing instruction is that tests and computerized scoring of student writing are making the "error hunt" (Weaver, 1996) the norm for writing instruction.

Atwood can serve us well if we hope to overcome these damning and discouraging facts about how we teach reading and writing in an increasingly prescriptive environment. For students to become empowered and authentic writers, both teachers and students need to understand and to experience *the writer's life* (Thomas, 2005b). That life includes discovering the answers to the following:

- How is a writer influenced by her *reading life?* What does it mean to *read like a writer?*
- What are authentic writing forms? How do writers choose those forms (genres)?
- What elements constitute the writing process of writers?
- How does choice impact the writer's life?

Here, we will look at Atwood's answers revealed in *Negotiating with the Dead.*

Atwood (2002) notes in her introduction the essential nature of being a writer:

> I am a writer and a reader, and that's about it. I'm not a scholar or a literary theoretician, and any such notions that have wandered into this book have got there by the usual writerly methods, which resemble the ways of the jackdaw: we steal the shiny bits, and build them into the structures of our own disorderly mess. (pp. xviii–xix)

This self-effacing comment raises a few concerns for those of us hoping to teach students to write—an ambition Kurt Vonnegut (1974) believes is fruitless. According to Atwood, writing appears to be mere thievery and middle school art methods. But writing is much more, and it can be fostered. The messages found in *Negotiating* include that the evolution of any writer is somewhat chaotic and easier to describe than to predict. Her introduction ends by suggesting that writing includes "darkness" and "desire" (p. xxiv); let's look briefly at how these elements can be addressed in our classes through this work.

"[W]riters tend to adopt their terms of discourse early in their reading and writing lives," Atwood (2002) believes; thus, we are pressed to offer the best reading and writing experiences we can in our classrooms (p. xxvi). Drawn from lectures on being a writer, Atwood offers the following key points about becoming and being a writer:

- Young writers are influenced heavily by "other people's biases about writers" (p. 5). I argue that how we as teachers portray writers directly and indirectly in our classes is crucial. To address the baggage our students carry into our classes concerning their perceptions of writers, we might begin our classes by asking students to brainstorm how they feel about and what they think of writers.

- Also key, according to Atwood, is the childhood of any writer; again, we can ask students to describe the reading and writing details of their own lives in their homes. Atwood loved comic books and other aspects of pop culture that clearly impacted her as a writer; she was also a voracious reader.

- One learns to write by writing—"All of this time I had been writing, compulsively, badly, hopefully," she confesses (p. 21). What students in our classes are relentless readers and writers but also hide these facts from peers and their teachers? How do we invite them to bring those facts of their lives into the classroom, into the light?

- In her first chapter, Atwood discusses her own journey from compulsive writer to a writer who submits and even publishes her work. For me there is a crucial point to be made here: *Our writing classrooms must rise above being places where writing is assigned and submitted for and to the teacher to becoming a place where young writers write by choice and for authentic purposes beyond the teacher and the classroom.*

- Chapter Two addresses the essential dual nature of being a writer. Atwood deals with dualities in many of her fictional works, but here we can bring to our classes questions about the various roles any writer plays during her or his writing process. Students should be asked to identify the various roles they play throughout their own writing process (which is also a process that is unique to each student and that each student must discover and refine; see Thomas, 2005b).

- The third chapter confronts students about literary worth—both the aesthetic worth and the monetary worth we place on art, specifically writing. For contemporary students steeped in materialistic lives, these are valuable and difficult considerations that profoundly impact how they view the value of writing and the value of themselves as writers.

ENTRY POINTS

In Chapter Three, Atwood references a number of works of literature that would work as wonderful entry points to a discussion of literary worth. One is John Keats' "Ode on a Grecian Urn," which raises essential questions about both the nature of art and the value in art. Elizabeth Barrett Browning's "A Musical Instrument" can serve as a nuanced view of art when paired with Keats' poem. She also mentions Franz Kafka's "A Fasting-Artist," a work that can serve as an exploration of the debate over art and how *popularity* impacts our view of that art.

CONNECTION

About "Hills like White Elephants," by Ernest Hemingway, Atwood explains, as a young reader, "I had no idea what the man and the woman were discussing" (p. 76). This story is an excellent work for exploring the qualities inherent in literature. Students can read and discuss this story in terms of Hemingway showing instead of telling; as well, students can discuss how literature addresses topics differently than other genres—such as an argument would discuss abortion directly. During the discussion, students can be asked to consider the purposes of literature specifically and of art broadly—notably issues dealing with theme, with popularity, and with reader enjoyment. In the chapter, Atwood mentions D. H. Lawrence and Oscar Wilde, writers who have received high literary praise while suffering varying degrees of social rejection and who highlight the tension surrounding literary worth.

- The next chapter discusses "the problem of moral and social responsibility," or the problem of politics within art (Atwood, 2002, p. 102). For students, the ways in which we address literature in school can often reduce literature to themes, suggesting that the themes (or political messages, for example) of art are more important than art. Here is a delicate discussion concerning the aims and goals of writers; it addresses the nature of craft in writing as it relates to the content. In short, just why do writers write?

Atwood's Chapter Four suggests an excellent unit to discuss the purpose of art within the political context. She notes the nature of Archibald MacLeish's poem "Ars Poetica," a poem that appears to say something contradictory through its message and its form. Then she contrasts MacLeish's poem to the work of Gertude Stein, who represents both a unique view about the nature of art and personifies the debate about how we should value writers who represent political and artistic agendas. Adrienne Rich, to whom Atwood turns at the end of the chapter, also embodies the artist who is identified strongly with political agendas and suffers negative commentary from more traditional critics because of that association.

- Writing very much like a teacher in her fifth chapter, Atwood addresses her upside-down V, the relationship among the writer, the reader, and the text (p. 125). For our classes, this is a crucial chapter because Atwood discusses the importance of the text because it is the only link between a reader and writer—emphasizing for our students *craft, audience,* and *purpose.* We might bring into class a comparison between Atwood's upside-down V with Rosenblatt's theory of the relationship among reader, writer, and text (Rosenblatt, 1995).
- Her final chapter comes back to her title for the book and her argument that writing "is motivated, deep down, by a fear of and fascination with mortality" (p. 156). She believes that writing shares with all art that urge to rise to immortality, but she distinguishes writing from other media by its ability to "survive as *voice*" (italics in original, p. 158). And for teachers of writing, we must be striving to help our students ultimately find their voices.

Near the end of this book (a great book for our students or an excellent source for us as we prepare to teach students to be writers), Atwood also circles back to the nature of writers: "And all must commit acts of larceny, or else of reclamation, depending on how you look at it" (p. 178). And in our classes, how *will* we look at it?

The Intent of the Writer— Atwood's Occasional Pieces

In *Writing with Intent,* Atwood (2005) notes that this collection of nonfiction "is an assemblage of occasional pieces—that is, pieces written for specific occasions" (p. xiii). At the end of the introduction, she returns to the title of the book: "But *intent* has other meanings. It can mean a state of mind or will, but it can also mean an inclination of spirit or soul. And, as a word, *intent* is joined at the hip with *intense*" (p. xvii). For me, this introduction and recent collection of essays offer a wealth of opportunities to help our students read with intent and write with intent—or, as I phrase it in my courses, with *purpose.*

This collection, more like *Second Words* than *Negotiating with the Dead,* includes reviews, essays, and speeches that can be brought into our classroom in a number of ways. In the following paragraphs, I discuss selected essays from the collection and how they might be added to our reading and writing curriculums. The end of this section emphasizes a number of Atwood's reviews of novels that should work as entry points for studying those novels in our classes.

"Laughter vs. Death" reads at times like a personal narrative and a discussion of her own journey in writing *Bodily Harm,* but the piece ultimately reveals itself as an argument—a passionate stance concerning the ill effects Atwood sees connected to violence in pornography. This is certainly a sensitive topic for the high school classroom, but helping students address issues of censorship and obscenity is a vital element of an education within a free society. Debates over censorship and obscenity (often directly about pornography) are perennial conflicts in American discourse and *about* our schools. Atwood's essay adds the nuance of her discussion growing from her experiences in a Canadian democracy, yet regardless of nation, freedom of expression is at the heart of any free society. She offers three ways to view pornography; as well, she helps show her readers how complex these debates are. This essay reveals an artist and writer toying with the value of state-mandated censorship. Beyond the controversial nature of this essay, Atwood also models for students that arguments often do not look as we prescribe them in school.

Despite Atwood's contention that her novels labeled as science fiction are *not* science fiction—which she explains well in this essay—"Writing Utopia" is a perfect essay for students to consider genre broadly and how we classify novels such as *The Handmaid's Tale* and *Oryx and Crake* specifically. Having read extensively and written about Kurt Vonnegut (Thomas, 2006), I recognize in both Vonnegut and Atwood a need to clarify their purposes as serious writers— complicated by their ambiguous feelings about genre labels. Our students need to be aware of the literary hierarchy that exists for genres; serious writers do not write "genre fiction"—sci-fi, romance, westerns, horror, and the like—but they may use those conventions in artistic ways within their serious fiction, goes the argument. In "Writing Utopia," the reader follows Atwood's argument that her speculative novel, *The Handmaid's Tale,* is in the utopia-dystopia tradition;

further, she explains that the novel fictionalizes what has happened and is happening in our world—not some future possibilities. We will return to this essay in Chapter Four.

Prose (2006) attempts to answer the question, "Can creative writing be taught?" (p. 8); this essay that discusses reading like a writer is a perfect companion to Atwood's "Nine Beginnings," which explores *"Why do you write?"* nine times. Here, students gain insight into both how writers read and write along with how writers view teaching and learning how to write. Prose's "Close Reading" also shares with Atwood's essay related discussions of all topics related to literature and the *love* writers feel for reading and books. In Prose's essay we hear an echo of Atwood's distrust of how education impacts a student's love of reading and writing: "Only once did my passion for reading steer me in the wrong direction, and that was when I let it persuade me to go to graduate school. There, I soon realized that my love for books was unshared by many of my classmates and professors" (p. 11). Yet, Atwood offers some compassion for struggling young writers in our classes since she shares that sense of struggle— "You begin again. It never gets any easier" (p. 110).

The nature of literature, the defining qualities of the novel, the portrayal of female characters in literature—all of these are central issues in our English classes as well as in Atwood's "Spotty-Handed Villainesses: Problems of Female Bad Behavior in the Creation of Literature." For the well-read student, this essay offers a wide range of references by Atwood, such as her use of Lady Macbeth and other female characters in Shakespeare to ground her discussion of portrayals of women in literature. After establishing her topics, Atwood echoes Barbara Kingsolver's comments about readers deriving fact from fiction but doubting any author's non-fiction accounts (Thomas, 2005a). Since this is one of the best-suited essays by Atwood to read and discuss in English classes, let me list some of the many topics she addresses:

- Early in the piece, Atwood argues "what novels are not" (p. 128). She also adds to this excellent discussion that students hold ideas about novels and novelists that are erroneous, blaming schools: "[H]ow does the novelist go about choosing [the plot]? Usually it's backward to what you were taught in school . . ." (p. 129).

- Atwood offers us as teachers opportunities to correct any misconceptions students have gathered from their schooling. Here, she discusses genre conventions and the role of conventions in the work of writers; writers purposefully work *within* conventions or *against* them, she explains. This understanding, as I have found when helping students grasp the use of technique in their work and that of established writers, is powerful and effective—particularly when this explanation replaces a "right/wrong" mentality about technique and convention.

- Students often miss essential information that we as adults assume all people know; in this essay, Atwood lists and discusses the Seven Deadly Sins, but I found that this term often meant nothing to my Advanced Placement students. Atwood allows us to discuss this classic information while also reconsidering how women are portrayed in literature.

- Determining meaning in a work of literature can prove to be quite complex; Atwood explains "what the character thinks is bad, what the reader thinks is bad, and what the author thinks is bad, may all be different" (p. 135)—and how does any reader (particularly a novice reader) sort all this out for a credible meaning?

- This piece can steer our students to works with much-persecuted female characters—Toni Morrison's *Beloved,* Thomas Hardy's *Tess of the D'Urbervilles,* Nathaniel Hawthorne's *The Scarlet Letter.* Further students can begin to discuss the role of the author's gender in the portrayal of women.

ENTRY POINT

In Atwood's "Spotty-Handed Villainesses," she raises the paradox of writers, and all artists, addressing the truth through the created, or what is essentially untrue. Early in the essay, she notes that writers are simply following the advice of Emily Dickinson's poem 1129 ("Tell all the Truth but tell it slant—"). This poem is a wonderful entry point into Atwood's essay and into a discussion of truth and writers portraying truth through poetry, fiction, and drama. "Success in Circuit lies," Dickinson suggests, with a brilliant use of ambiguity in the word "lies" while discussing truth (1. 2); as well, Dickinson directly addresses the need for slowly revealed truth for children in particular—a topic that should be of interest to high school and college students who are transitioning from the highly allegorical world of the child to the brutally frank world of adulthood. (This may be an interesting topic when using children's literature in our classes; see Chapter Eight for that discussion.)

"Would I have written the book if I never visited Afghanistan? Possibly. Would it have been the same? Unlikely" ends Atwood's "When Afghanistan Was at Peace," a brief essay that details some of her visit to the country and how that impacted her writing *The Handmaid's Tale* (p. 207). As the U.S. military involvement in the Middle East grows, our students need ample opportunities to explore and understand the geography, the history, the politics, and the complexity of the Middle East. This essay introduces students to some of the customs of Afghanistan, notably among the women, as Atwood writes of buying a chador (a traditional garment for women) and how she incorporated such customs into her dystopian novel.

Another brief and thought-provoking piece is her "Letter to America," which raises her concerns about the U.S. from an outsider who is intimately familiar with the country. While the content of the essay can be useful in our classroom discussions, I would suggest allowing students to borrow the format, writing letters to the U.S.—or other countries—as a way to explore their attitudes toward their homeland and to other countries. Another valuable aspect of the essay for our English courses is Atwood's listing of the people she associates with American thought, people she admires—such as Emily Dickinson, Henry David Thoreau, and Arthur Miller. On one hand, we do often portray the people she notes as central to traditional American beliefs and ideals, but on the other hand, I would challenge students to confront whether or not these people and ideas are truly what Americans embrace. In my American Literature course, students and I often discussed the contrast between what we associate with writers and thinkers such as Henry David Thoreau, Ralph Waldo Emerson, and Margaret Fuller with the ideals average Americans actually practice.

The final piece I highly recommend is Atwood's "George Orwell: Some Personal Connections." This essay offers wonderful reflections by Atwood on her own reading past while introducing students to the brilliant and highly relevant ideas of writer George Orwell. She understands the qualities of children as readers as well as teens as readers—concepts both students and teachers should explore. But the ideas she extracts from the works of Orwell are the central reasons this essay should be added to our classrooms. "As Orwell taught, it isn't the labels . . . that are definitive, but the acts done in their name"—this and other such points about the nature of ideology and the use of language for power and control are all vital discussions that must occur in English classrooms where confronting the text and confronting the world are valued (p. 288). Much as Orwell does, Atwood shines a bright light on the paradoxes of power and the powerful, those who champion certain ideals in their words while negating the parallel realities with their actions. Ultimately, Atwood and Orwell serve us well in the English classroom because they stress the importance of language in the real lives of all people who are striving to be free.

Atwell's "George Orwell" is an excellent entry point into *Animal Farm* (as a first-time reading or as a re-reading since we often assign this work too early in students' reading lives) and *1984*. While the essay reveals a great deal about Atwood herself, it is also a micro-primer into the ideas of Orwell. That the piece acknowledges layers of understanding when faced with Orwell's work throughout a young reader's life is also an added benefit of reading the essay in our classes before beginning to explore Orwell.

Another excellent use of essays in this collection is that the many book reviews by Atwood can be used as models for students either to write their own authentic book reviews or as entry points into the works and writers she reviews. Some of these works and writers I have found effective in my classes are:

- John Updike—Atwood reviews *The Witches of Eastwick,* but Updike offers a wide range of genres suitable for the classroom; many of his short stories have worked extremely well in classes.
- Italo Calvino—Calvino is one of many well-respected authors we tend to ignore, but whose work would breathe life into an often-stale canon.
- Toni Morrison—Morrison's *Beloved* is reviewed; her *Song of Solomon* is another excellent work that has been embraced by my students.
- Gabriel Garcia Marquez—As with Calvino, Marquez provides us with wonderful writing that expands the types of works we bring to our students, notably voices outside of North America and Europe.
- Virginia Woolf—The use of Woolf in our classrooms has probably fluctuated throughout the past few decades, but her work remains important and needed for our students.

Many other writers and works are reviewed by Atwood, all of whom would be excellent additions to our reading lists. Since Atwood offers so many reviews, they might be used as ways to allow students guided choice in their reading by having students read these reviews and picking among those books for a reason.

In Her Own Words—Atwood's Interviews

In our English classrooms, we commonly focus our energy on the carefully composed word—either analyzing a writer's text or shaping an original text in multiple drafts. The interview is a common aspect of communication in our visual and aural media age; as well, interviewing artists is a common way to make us feel we are closer to the artist. The interview fits well into our contemporary obsessions with celebrity.

Margaret Atwood: Conversations was published in 1990 and contains twenty-one interviews with Atwood, some by Graeme Gibson and Joyce Carol Oates, adding some nuance to our interest in the interviews. I recommend using her interviews or sections of her interviews because they provide transcripts of somewhat organic discussions of Atwood as a writer and of how she approaches her own work (and the reactions of others to her work). The rhythm of Atwood's spontaneous comments does allow the students some insight to her as a person and may allow them the opportunity to compare that to Atwood the writer. This is important, I believe, because many people are unable or unwilling to separate the persona of a writer or artist from the larger (and often much more complex) person.

This collection also includes a great deal of commentary on Atwood's works into the middle period of her career, notably through the publication of *The Handmaid's Tale.* The interaction, again, between the interviewer and Atwood offers a layer of discussion and analysis that traditional critical essays cannot. What often strikes me while reading these interviews is Atwood's tendency to reveal frustration and even irritation at the assumptions and suggestions clothed in the interviewer's comment and questions. Woven into the discussion of Atwood and her works are excellent considerations of other writers, of being a writer, of genre, of gender, and of politics—all the elements that characterize Atwood's polished writing.

CONNECTION

An excellent full-length interview available in text and on video/DVD is *The Power of Myth,* an interview by Bill Moyers with comparative religion and mythology scholar Joseph Campbell. This interview portrays a similar complexity and richness found in many of the interviews with Atwood, and Campbell's Jungian lens for all things fits well with the mythological patterns running through Atwood's work.

These interviews could also support a mini-unit on preparing for and conducting interviews. Students could interview each other or select someone else to interview. The assignment should include some requirements that they prepare for the interview, which may serve as a much more authentic form of research when compared to the traditional research paper assignment prepared simply for the teacher. Of course, many students may be more motivated by an assignment that is language rich but requires the use of video equipment and other technology.

This chapter has several arguments. First, I continue to stress the need for our classrooms to increase the amount of nonfiction proportionately to the amount of fiction and poetry we read and write about in English classes. Simply put, nonfiction is undervalued in schools. Next, I do believe that the nonfiction of Margaret Atwood is an excellent way to address that imbalance, both as an addition to the reading of our courses and as models for our students' own essay writing. Finally, I believe we need to expand the range of nonfiction our students write while also making our teaching and their learning more authentic in terms of how nonfiction looks when practiced by published authors.

In Chapter Three, I turn to discussing some of the early novels of Atwood, such as *The Edible Woman, Surfacing, Lady Oracle,* and *Bodily Harm.*

ENTRY POINTS AND CONNECTIONS

The Passion of Emily Dickinson, Judith Farr

Telling Women's Lives: The New Biography, Linda Wagner-Martin

Vertigo, Louise DeSalvo

"Ode on a Grecian Urn," John Keats

"A Musical Instrument," Elizabeth Barrett Browning

"A Fasting-Artist," Franz Kafka

"Hills like White Elephants," Ernest Hemingway

"Ars Poetica," Archibald MacLeish

Gertrude Stein

Adrienne Rich

("Tell all the Truth but tell it slant—"), Emily Dickinson [poem 1129]

Animal Farm, 1984, George Orwell

The Power of Myth, Joseph Campbell with Bill Moyers

Chapter Three

Early Novels

A Woman, an Artist, a Canadian

"I haven't worked this out," explained Atwood (Ingersoll, 1990), continuing, "I just can't be that analytical about my own work. . . . I know by the logic of the book what they are doing, but I don't have a whole lot of theories about it. They exist. You can make of it what you will" (p. 18). As a writer, Atwood is allowed this ambivalence about trying to discern meaning from her fiction. As teachers and students, however, we are often, if not drawn to being analytical, required to mine novels for meaning.

For our purposes here, I am addressing her novels in groups—in this chapter, the early novels she published from 1970 until 1976, *The Edible Woman, Surfacing,* and *Lady Oracle.* While Stein (1999) groups the novels somewhat differently than I do (placing Atwood's first six novels in two groups of three by chronology), she explains that the first three novels include qualities that Atwood expands upon in her next three novels (I save *Bodily Harm, Life Before Man,* and *The Handmaid's Tale* for a chapter with *Oryx and Crake* since they share dystopian patterns). Stein believes Atwood demonstrates in these early works her gifts as a writer—as a writer who happens to be female and Canadian.

Cooke (2004) explains that Atwood's early works establish "three different impulses driving [her] fiction (feminist, nationalist, and postmodern) and their corresponding themes (women, Canada and the preservation of its wildness, and writing)" (p. 29). The early novels are important for our students, Cooke argues, since they provide a foundation for "understanding . . . Atwood's larger project" (p. 29).

Here, I discuss these three novels in terms of how they might fit our classes during study of the novel and in a variety of ways for our reading and writing curriculum.

The Edible Woman—The Lives of Women in a Consumer Society

Stein (1999) and Cooke (2004) both recognize the satirical strengths of Atwood's first published novel—a work that explores Atwood's view of consumer society's negative impact on women. The novel explores "the way society has institutionalized methods of marginalizing and disempowering women," explains Cooke (p. 31). The satire, the feminist perspective unique to Atwood, and the characterization in the novel all make this novel an excellent choice for our classroom, particularly if we are introducing these qualities to students.

In the novel, the main character, Marian MacAlpin, struggles with her appetite for both men and food as she works as a market researcher in early 1960s Toronto. Her problems with men and food combined with her experiences at Seymour Surveys provide a platform for Atwood to explore and readers to consider the condition of being female in a modern world characterized by consumerism. What makes Atwood's considerations ideal for the classroom is captured by Stein (1999): "Her books raise feminist and other political issues, but their voices are always plural and dialogic, questioning more than they answer and often interrogating feminism as well as other social ideologies and practices" (p. 44).

CONNECTION

Cooke (2004) suggests that *The Edible Woman* is rooted in Atwood's 1963–1964 job for Canadian Facts Marketing. Atwood satirizes the consumer mentality along with aspects of the corporate world. Kurt Vonnegut's first novel, *Player Piano*, confronted many of the same elements nearly two decades prior to Atwood's first novel—in his own first novel. Vonnegut's novel works well as a companion work to Atwood's *The Edible Woman* since the two works share many qualities but have a number of distinct perspectives. The nuanced feminist views of Atwood provide readers and students with an additional lens for examining Vonnegut's criticism of corporate dynamics.

Students can be led to approach the novel through a series of broad questions; some of which are as follows:

- How does Atwood use a food motif to organize her novel? What does this motif suggest about eating disorders such as anorexia? How is a dramatization of Marian's eating disorder through fiction different than other explorations of anorexia such as a documentary or the interview of an actual person who has suffered from the disease?

CONNECTION

Stein (1999) and Cooke (2004) recognize elements from *Alice in Wonderland* in *The Edible Woman*. The food and eating motifs owe a great deal to this well-known story. Cooke notes that Atwood's dinner scene in Chapter 22 parallels the Mad Hatter's tea party, for example. Students can be asked to find the parallels, and then they should explain how these parallels contribute to Atwood's novel.

- Related to Marian's eating disorder are Atwood's questions concerning the portrayal of body images in a consumer society. How does advertising portray bodies through billboards and magazines? Are those portrayals and their impacts the same or different for men and women? How does Atwood dramatize these portrayals? Are the ideal body images in today's consumer society unique when compared to other societies throughout history?
- How is clothing significant in the novel and in our society? How is it connected to issues of gender between the male and female characters? How does the clothing support Atwood's characterization?
- What is a feminist perspective? How does Atwood weave a feminist perspective into her fiction? How is Atwood's portrayal of feminism unique?

CONNECTION

Stein (1999) places Atwood's novel directly after Betty Friedan's *The Feminine Mystique* and Sylvia Plath's *The Bell Jar.* A paired novel unit of *The Edible Woman* and *The Bell Jar* can be an effective way to introduce students to feminism as a movement and as a critical lens when approaching art. Stein identifies several parallels in Atwood's work and Plath's work. One key distinction, however, is that the two novels have different conclusions. Students may begin to realize that a perspective, such as a feminist perspective, is not a unified thing.

- Cooke (2004) raises an excellent point about the characters in Atwood's novel: "However, in such early novels as *The Edible*

Woman, the charge that male characters seem rather flat and two-dimensional seems justified" (p. 46). Is the characterization in Atwood's novel fully developed, particularly the male characters as compared to the female? If the male characters are under-developed, two-dimensional, does this detract from the quality of the novel or of Atwood as a writer?

CONNECTION

The importance of characterization is stressed by fiction writer John Gardner. His short story, "Redemption," is a tour de force of characterization in a brief piece of fiction; he also touches on eating disorders in the reaction of the mother in the story to the death of her son in a tragic farming accident.

- What characterizes a consumer society? What are the positive and negative influences of a consumer society? What does Atwood suggest about consumerism in her novel? How does she specifically comment on the effects of consumerism on women?
- What narrative technique carries the three sections of the novel? Why does Atwood shift the narration among the three sections?

A novel that questions is fertile ground for an English course; beyond these central questions, one other aspect of this novel and most of Atwood's works can serve as an instructional focus—her use of mythic patterns. The Greek myth of Persephone can be found in many of Atwood's works, throughout genres, and it is central to *The Edible Woman:* "[Marian] thus takes on the role of Persephone, pursued by a deathlike suitor (and indeed, she descends into a maze symbolic of the underworld)," explains Stein (1999, p. 44).

The myth of Persephone proves to be a complex one, including the varied and diverse associations with the character and the myth. Atwood's works embrace such ambiguities, notably in her approach to the condition of women. As I have noted earlier, Atwood (Snell, 1997) rejects a simplistic view of women as victims—although many critics still explain her work in those terms. Further, Atwood typically incorporates *and* manipulates traditional techniques and ideas—as with her use of mythic patterns.

While this first novel by Atwood can stand on its own, it can also serve as an excellent introduction to many of her works. Let's now look at her second novel, *Surfacing.*

Surfacing—Journeys of Self-discovery

From her earliest works, Atwood demonstrates a writer's ability to work within a convention while also deconstructing that convention (often through satire)—leaving readers and critics to wrestle with her ambiguity. In *Surfacing,* she continues to explore feminist issues while she "introduces the theme of Canadian nationalism and corresponding concerns about the preservation of the Canadian wilderness" (Cooke, 2004, p. 53). For our classrooms, *Surfacing* provides an excellent opportunity to discuss a work of self-discovery as well as an avenue to consider nationalism.

Since adolescence is a time of heightened concerns about Self, a literature unit on self-discovery is often engaging for students in high school and college. *Surfacing* offers students the dramatization of the novel's unnamed narrator as she looks deeply into her own self; this work also adds to the classroom the journey of a woman—as a counter-balance to the numerous works about this same journey by men. Cooke (2004) details the theme of self-discovery in the novel and mentions a number of related works on a similar theme; with her suggestions in mind, I am including here a potential list of works to create a unit on self-discovery:

- *On the Road,* Jack Kerouac—This masculine journey is alluded to in the opening of *Surfacing* (Cooke, 2004, p. 54) and can serve as a contrast to Atwood's work. How does Atwood write within the traditions of works about self-discovery and how does she push against those same traditions?
- *The Bean Trees,* Barbara Kingsolver—The journey motif drives this first novel by Kingsolver (Thomas, 2005a) and would fit well as a companion novel to *Surfacing* in a unit on self-discovery.
- *The Awakening,* Kate Chopin—Kingsolver's and Kerouac's novels have literal journeys central to their works; Chopin's work can be described as more of a psychological journey, which parallels the same awakening found in Atwood's work. A nuance added by *The Awakening* is that Chopin's work was written about seven decades before Atwood's, revealing the evolving feminist perspective for our students.
- *The Golden Notebook,* Doris Lessing—Cooke (2004) believes this novel, published a decade before Atwood's, would be a valuable novel to compare journeys of self-discovery (p. 67).
- *Their Eyes Were Watching God,* Zora Neale Hurston—While the works suggested so far add complexity to the theme of self-discovery in terms of gender and history, Hurston's work adds the element of race.

A novel unit on self-discovery with *Surfacing* as an anchoring work could be implemented in many ways. All of our students could read and discuss *Surfacing* as a whole-class activity, then students might be broken into small groups and choose or be assigned the novels above (or numerous other works) with a focus on how these other works add to the theme of self-discovery. Each small group could work independently with a project and presentation due at the end and to be shared with the whole group.

ENTRY POINT

Cooke (2004) identifies Adrienne Rich's "Diving into the Wreck" as sharing imagery and themes with *Surfacing.* This wonderful and complex poem by Rich would be an excellent entry point into the novel and the unit on self-discovery. Through the poem, students could begin to explore the imagery of diving found both in the poem and the novel, themes related to feminism, themes related to self-discovery, and both Freudian and Jungian elements.

CONNECTION

Stein (1999) explains that "[a]s the protagonist moves from a corrupt and alienating city to her family's island cabin, her journey mirrors the Demeter-Persephone myth, a tale of death and rebirth, of the separation and reunion of mother and daughter" (p. 52). The introduction of the Demeter-Persephone myth for students reinforces the discussion about Jungian elements commonly found in Atwood, whose work is rich with mythic structures that allow her to confront traditional assumptions.

A novel unit on self-discovery for high school and college students can be as much a personal as an academic experience. The ability of our students to have complex analytical reactions to literature along with nuanced personal responses can be addressed through this unit (Rosenblatt, 1995). This theme lends itself to rich writing experiences as well. Some writing assignments well suited to this unit include:

- Personal narratives and memoirs are some of the best writing assignments I have found. These forms lend themselves to students discussing their own journeys to self-discovery. *Surfacing* explores the narrator's struggles with her mother and father as part of her journey—a topic that is fresh on the minds of students in high school and college as they are facing the inevitable break with home. This familial theme is found in *The Glass Menagerie, Death of a Salesman, The Catcher in the Rye, Ordinary People,* and many young adult novels.

- Poetry, such as Rich's "Diving into the Wreck," can serve as an artistic expression of self-discovery that is not bound by the facts of our students' lives, as in personal narrative and memoir, but is guided by the personal realizations that often prove to be universal. A poetry workshop associated with this unit could ask students to make their self-discoveries public through imagery and mythic patterns, both modeled in Atwood and Rich.

- Literary analysis remains a traditional goal of our English courses, particularly for students in advanced courses. On many assessments of a student's ability to analyze literature, prompts require that student to compare and contrast more than one work. The unit outlined above could include asking students to compare *Surfacing* with the other novel in their small group.

Surfacing is much more than a novel of self-discovery; it also confronts Canadian nationalism and nationalism as a concept. Within this focus of the novel, Atwood also asks the reader to look closely at themes addressing wilderness and industrialization (and commercialism), particularly in the context of contrasting the United States with Canada. In the novel, Atwood personifies her concern for nature and the wilderness in American characters who are "threatening and thoughtless" (Cooke, 2004, p. 60) and in her rich description of the wilderness that is much of Canada. Cooke notes that this pattern can be found in many of Atwood's poems as well—"It is Dangerous to Read Newspapers," "Trainride, Vienna-Bonn," "At the Tourist Center in Boston" (pp. 60, 65).

For me, these elements in *Surfacing* are excellent opportunities to ask students to consider political arguments that are not bound by simple differences between political parties. The politics of this novel confronts the dangers and promises of nationalism as well as the threats humanity poses for itself in our careless attitudes toward nature. For many of our students, the twenty-first century is a time when we continue to debate nationalistic pride in the face of terrorism *and* argue seriously about our duty to the planet as it relates to our consumption of natural resources (such as oil products at the center of that same war on terror).

CONNECTION

Before he gained recognition for *Fahrenheit 9/11*, Michael Moore explored the United States' obsession with guns and contrasted that national identity with

Canadian attitudes in *Bowling for Columbine* (2002). This work garnered an Academy Award for Best Documentary, but it attracts a great deal of criticism from many who feel that Moore produces more fiction than nonfiction. Regardless of the political stances of our students, this film is a perfect companion to *Surfacing* since it forces the viewer to consider similar themes about the US and Canada in the context of national identities. As well, Moore tends to characterize Americans as Atwood does in her novel—as careless and aggressive. Moore also has web-based resources for studying the documentary (available at http://www.bowlingforcolumbine.com/).

ENTRY POINT

Canadian poet Gwendolyn MacEwen writes, "This land like a mirror turns you inward/ And you become a forest in a furtive lake" (11. 1–2) in her "Dark Pines Under Water." Myers (2004) connects MacEwen's exploration with Atwood's *Surfacing* as works exploring both self and Canada. As well, these works share imagery, the lake and sinking/diving into that lake.

Surfacing proves to be a rich and engaging work in the classroom. In addition to the broader focuses offered above, this novel addresses a number of other topics that could prove to be valuable units and assignments as well; let's look at a few here briefly:

- Inherent in Atwood's exploration of self-discovery is the narrator's wrestling with her own parents, their lives and her perception of their lives: "Indeed she becomes increasingly introspective, daily activities triggering memories of her childhood," explains Cooke (2004, p. 57).

CONNECTION

The narrator of *Surfacing* struggles with the sanity of her father and her own responsibility toward the privacy of his life and his art. In *Proof* (a fine play by David Auburn and subsequent movie starring Gwyneth Paltrow and Anthony Hopkins), the daughter faces a similar struggle that contributes to her own self-discovery and rebirth. The movie version of *Proof* is well acted and written; it should be an excellent companion work to *Surfacing* as we seek to explore broader understandings of literacy, including visual literacy. Both works present characters facing the mortality of their parents.

- Abortion politics simmered beneath the surface of the world within which Atwood wrote the novel—the late 1960s and early 1970s. The unnamed narrator also struggles throughout the novel with her own abortion. In the three decades since *Roe v. Wade* in the United States, the abortion debate and the related polarizing language within that debate are still common in the lives of our students.

- Victimization and survival are thematic concerns found in this novel and thematic concerns Atwood addresses with a great deal of complexity. Both victimization and survival are issues of power and empowerment that are central to Atwood's unique feminist perspective. Atwood's work argues for a self-empowerment that acknowledges the imbalance of power between men and women, between humanity and nature, between the U.S. and Canada, but she also argues for the ability of all people to empower themselves by rejecting their role as victim.

- Cooke (2004) notes that Atwood's *Surfacing* includes writer's craft worth noting in our courses—the "unreliable narrator and her use of poetry in a work of prose fiction" (p. 69). The use of the unreliable narrator is often associated with modern works; students commonly read Twain and address this technique. Atwood's blending of genres, however, is less often explored in our classes.

- While I have identified this novel as a quest narrative, critics have called the novel a detective novel, and Atwood has characterized her work as a ghost story. Students can explore this novel as a discussion of conventional forms of genre.

Surfacing establishes the female artist as a character in Atwood's works; she focuses on this theme and expands it greatly in her next novel, *Lady Oracle*.

Portrait of the Artist as a Young Woman— *Lady Oracle* and One Person's Many Lives

Cooke (2004) identifies *Lady Oracle* as the first work by Atwood to focus on "a third, and central, and recurring theme of Atwood's work: writing" (p. 79). This novel, published in 1976, explores fully the life of the artist, in terms of the artist being a woman and in terms of how our modern societies respond to pop art and serious art (and whether or not such a distinction is even fair or accurate). The novel opens with an ominous and complex statement about the main character's life and death: "I planned my death carefully; unlike my life, which meandered along from one thing to another, despite my feeble attempts to control it" (p. 7). Here, readers begin to recognize the Atwood of later works as she continues to experiment with the many different versions of a person's life and the many levels of truths within those stories.

For our classrooms, *Lady Oracle* offers opportunities to address genre—specifically Atwood's manipulation of romance fiction and her working within and against the conventions of gothic novels. Further, this work offers students opportunities to discuss two major themes running through the novel—the nature and perceptions of art, and the allure and evasiveness of escape. Atwood addresses all of these both directly and through humor, making the work ideal in many ways for the classroom.

Told in a non-linear structure by the main character, Joan Foster (who writes gothic novels under the pen-name Louisa K. Delacourt), the novel is a confession of sorts by Joan to a newspaper reporter who uncovers her faked suicide and thus her many different lives: "The novel itself is a series of stories within the framework of Joan's story as told to a newspaper reporter" (Stein, 1999, p. 59). In essence, Atwood has the main character create many lives for herself; then Atwood places Joan in a circumstance where she is forced to *retell* all of those lives—raising a number of questions about narrative and about narrative truth (relative to perspective). Surrounding all of the other elements we can discuss in our classes through this novel has a central concern for writing, storytelling, language, and truth—all vital issues to be raised in our English classes.

First, let's consider addressing romance and romance narratives through *Lady Oracle*. The romance narrative is one that virtually all students know—and even enjoy through popular culture (which we will address later). From children's literature to TV shows to popular movies, our students have some concept of the romance template—which includes the knight in shining armor motif. Before reading the novel, students should revisit either *Cinderella* or *Rapunzel*—both common in our experiences through Disney and Grimms's Fairy Tales. These stories can refresh our students' awareness of a romance pattern; as well, the many versions of these classic stories can introduce students to multiple narratives, which Atwood explores in her novel.

The fairy tale opening should ask students to consider the following:

- What story pattern do *Cinderella* and *Rapunzel* share? Can you chart that pattern?
- What do these fairy tales assume about the roles of women? How are women characterized?
- What do these fairy tales assume about the roles of men (as princes)? How are men characterized?
- Do you know of any current movie or TV show that follows that same pattern?

Although carrying an R rating, the popular movie *Pretty Woman,* starring Julia Roberts and Richard Gere, offers a modern rendition of the knight-in-shining armor motif. This movie can be an interesting connection to *Lady Oracle* and the discussion of romance narratives. Particularly engaging is the debate concerning whether or not the movie is essentially a copy of *Cinderella* or if the movie has a twist on what we expect in that motif. Students should be asked if the Roberts character actually rescues the Gere character, a reversal of the classic form. Students should be asked to consider how this movie version of the romance narrative portrays the roles of men and women.

In *Lady Oracle,* Atwood models and confronts both romance motifs and gothic elements through the main narrative and the italicized passages from the novels written by Joan as Louisa K. Delacourt. After students consider and reconsider the fairy tale versions of romance, we should introduce them to the gothic elements found in classic works such as Mary Shelley's *Frankenstein,* Charles Dickens's *Great Expectations,* Emily Bronte's *Wuthering Heights,* or William Faulkner's *Absalom! Absalom!* (Cooke, 2004, p. 94). From a series of convoluted romances to ghosts and other apparitions to faked deaths and multiple lives, *Lady Oracle* works within gothic and romance traditions while also holding those traditions up for satire.

Since *Lady Oracle* demands a great deal of its reader—knowledge of many conventions and the ability to sift through Atwood's satire—students often find films more engaging avenues to the complexities of satire. Mel Brooks's classic comedy *Young Frankenstein* parallels Atwood's novel in its use of and parody of gothic elements; further, the novel is enhanced if the viewer is familiar with the original story of Dr. Frankenstein and his creation. Rated PG, the film is suitable for classes even in early high school; this film can be useful when we discuss popular art and high art, also addressed by Atwood in this novel.

Rosenblatt (1995) argues for a balance in teacher expectations for students' responses to literature—a balance between academic and personal responses. On a personal level, why would a student care about these issues of romance, gothic elements, and satire? Cooke (2004) explains that "Atwood, through Joan, illustrates the dangers of gothic thinking" (p. 95). Adolescents in high school and college are often blinded by their romantic (or idealistic) views of the world. And Cooke's analysis of *Lady Oracle* suggests the novel is an ideal means of asking students about their own views of the world, love and relationships, and their futures.

A central element running through the gothic nature of the novel is the Fat Lady: "The Fat Lady seems to haunt Joan's novel" and her life, notes Cooke (2004, p. 86). *Lady Oracle* includes ghost elements in a variety of ways, but the Fat Lady that recurs in Joan's life and her writing grows from her own image of herself as an obese child; Joan comes to realize "that thin women and fat women are treated entirely differently" (Cooke, p. 81). Many of Atwood's works address issues of body image and eating disorders in women; as noted above, this topic is relevant to the personal lives of our students. Yet, Atwood's use of the Fat Lady motif offers many avenues for the classroom, including a fairly rich allusive quality.

ENTRY POINT

Again mixing humor and serious topics in film, *Shallow Hal,* a fairly recent movie by gross-out directors Bobby and Peter Farrelly, offers a perceptive and well-acted movie about how we view people—notably women—and how we judge people based on physical appearance. This movie stars Jack Black and Gwyneth Paltrow, depending on a great deal of physical humor surrounding Black's character "seeing" a thin Paltrow character who is actually quite obese; part of the controversial humor revolves around that the viewers are allowed to see the obese Patrow character (who is stunningly transformed in a "fat" suit, reminiscent of real-life body transformations in Hollywood by Charlize Theron and Robert De Niro—also fertile ground for classroom discussions) that the Black character does not see until the end.

CONNECTIONS

The small canon of works by J. D. Salinger creates its own internal mythology anchored by the suicide of the spiritual and troubled Seymour Glass, whose moral vision and parable-rich messages guide and haunt his family after his death. In *Franny and Zooey,* these two stories originally published in *The New Yorker* culminate in a central motif of Salinger's writing and of the Glass family mythology—the Fat Lady. Franny and Zooey share an epiphany that Seymour's parable of the Fat Lady is a message about "'Christ Himself'"—as "Zooey" ends with Franny trapped in her own spiritual crisis. Sharing Atwood's Canadian heritage and Salinger's use of initials, W. P. Kinsella alludes to Salinger's Fat Lady motif in his short story, "The Night Manny Mota Tied the Record." Kinsella, well-known for his novel that inspired Kevin Costner's *Field of Dreams, Shoeless Joe,* offers a parallel consideration of moral dilemmas in his baseball story with his own use of the Fat Lady. Both or either of these works fits well with *Lady Oracle;* further, Salinger and Kinsella are often accused of using the Fat Lady motif in a misogynistic way, more endorsing society's attitude toward obesity in women than confronting that attitude. For our students, Atwood's use of the same Fat Lady motif allows them to discuss and debate if and how all three authors use this image.

As I noted in the beginning of this section on *Lady Oracle,* Atwood is concerned with writing, with art, and with women as artists in this work. Cooke (2004) recognizes that the Fat Lady motif intertwines with the writing motif: "Two of Joan's identities haunt her . . . : her writing self and her former, fat self, whose body she still sees in the mirror" (p. 84). Many debates and clarifications can come from these topics as our students read this work; we might raise the following points:

- Joan experiences automatic writing in one chapter and the result alludes to Tennyson's "The Lady of Shalott," a work that also addresses perceptions and views of women as well as the role of artists in society (Cooke, 2004). Comparing Tennyson's poem with Atwood's novel allows students to discuss the similarities and differences of artistic explorations of these themes by a male and a female writer and by writers separated by time.

- Automatic writing as a topic in the novel serves as a wonderful focus of debate about art. Automatic writing is associated with unconscious creativity and is, of course, rich with controversy. As both an artistic and psychiatric movement, automatic writing can be researched by students and debated as whether or not it is art— or even real. Related to this is the literary debate about the Beat Writers, such as Jack Kerouac and Allen Ginsberg. Many Beat Writers claimed to write in somewhat manic states that included little or no revision. Here, *Lady Oracle* can provide an excellent entry to debating the nature of art and the tension between how we distinguish popular art from high (or serious) art. For example, how is Atwood's novel, *Lady Oracle,* distinguishable—if at all—from the novels-within-the-novel of her main character?

CONNECTION

Raising many of the same topics and themes concerning high art, popular art, and the role of gender in the perception of artists in society, Kurt Vonnegut's *Bluebeard* is a dynamic companion novel to Atwood's *Lady Oracle,* especially since

Bluebeard is one of few works by Vonnegut given credit for exploring well issues related to women (Thomas, 2006). Vonnegut's novel also shares with Atwood the use of humor on serious topics.

- -

Related to writing but also moving beyond that topic into the novel's consideration of escape (or the inability for anyone to escape, as Joan is discovered in her attempt to fake her death and start anew) is Atwood's poetry. In "This Is a Photograph of Me" and "Siren Song," Atwood includes a portrayal of self-created imprisonments similar to the events of Joan's life in *Lady Oracle* (Cooke, 2004, p. 92). In the poems and the novel, Atwood raises the question: Do we create the prison from which we attempt to escape? For adolescents in high school and college, this question is often quite real as they are transitioning from artificial limitations (in their eyes) into an idealized freedom they associate with leaving school and entering the "real" world.

With those last words—"the 'real' world"—ringing in our readers' ears, let's move into Atwood's dystopian novels, where she creates alternate worlds to comment upon this world in which we live.

Entry Points and Connections

Player Piano, Kurt Vonnegut

Alice in Wonderland, Lewis Carroll

The Bell Jar, Sylvia Plath

"Redemption," John Gardner

"Diving into the Wreck," Adrienne Rich

Demeter-Persephone Myth

Bowling for Columbine, Michael Moore, dir.

"Dark Pines Under Water," Gwendolyn MacEwen

Proof, John Madden, dir.; David Auburn, screenplay/play

Pretty Woman, Garry Marshall, dir.

Young Frankenstein, Mel Brooks, dir.

Shallow Hal, Bobby and Peter Farrelly, dirs.

Franny and Zooey, J. D. Salinger

"The Night Manny Mota Tied the Record," W. P. Kinsella

Bluebeard, Kurt Vonnegut

Chapter Four

Dark and Speculative (Dystopian) Novels

In the popular movie *Notting Hill,* William (Hugh Grant) has trouble climbing over a fence into a private garden; Anna (Julia Roberts) climbs in seemingly effortlessly. William stumbles and nearly falls. Once inside the garden, William says, "Now what in the world in this garden could make that ordeal worthwhile?"—prompting a kiss from Anna, to which he says, "Nice garden."

Such are the idealistic gardens of popular romance, but Margaret Atwood offers us no such idyllic settings and plots. Yet, her works are often filled with *seeming* gardens that hide much darker realities. Her *Life Before Man* (1979), *Bodily Harm* (1981), and *The Handmaid's Tale* (1985) are all grouped as similar works in terms of their dystopias and "nightmarish world[s]" (Cooke, 2004, p. 113). Atwood and critics (Stein, 1999; Cooke) recognize these similarities, which are also dominant in *Oryx and Crake* (2003). Here, we explore these four novels as works addressing interrelated themes and motifs— imprisonment, dystopias, science and technology threatening nature and humanity, sexual politics, government, pornography, women's friendships, and narrators as "storyteller[s], witness[es], and reporter[s]" (Stein, p. 65).

ENTRY POINTS

Critical discussions of Atwood's works, including the four novels we address in this chapter, always include Atwood's wrestling with genre. Both Atwood and

Kurt Vonnegut have written and spoken often about the misrepresentations their works often endure. These two authors share a tendency to refute—or to at least clarify—the labeling of their works as "science fiction" and "dystopian literature." In Vonnegut's "Science Fiction," students can analyze Vonnegut's realization that *he* had been labeled a writer of science fiction, leading to his acknowledging such as a negative label and to his clever remarks about whether or not Franz Kafka wrote science fiction. Atwood's "Writing Utopia" is a more complex and well-thought-out piece that explores genre along with whether or not *The Handmaid's Tale* should be labeled science fiction or a dystopian work. This essay is ideal for a unit including any of the four novels discussed in this chapter or for a unit on *The Handmaid's Tale*.

Although *Life Before Man* and *Bodily Harm* are distinct from *The Handmaid's Tale* and *Oryx and Crake* in terms of time—the first two set in contemporary times and the second two set in the future—these works explore the dark realities that face humanity, often specifically women as imprisoned in dark political realities. Whether taught within a unit of more than one of these novels or individually, these four works offer rich opportunities for addressing genre, the novel form, and a wide range of complex themes and motifs in our high school and college English courses.

Dark Reality—*Life Before Man*

How do I place a realistic novel about a love triangle, set in contemporary Canada, in a chapter on dystopian works by Atwood? Stein (1999) explains that, primarily, "*Life Before Man* uses realism to undercut it" (p. 70). This novel's motifs and themes combined with Atwood's manipulation of realistic conventions create a work that appears to be something that it proves not to be—much as the alluring gardens of these novels hide much darker realities.

The novel covers about two years and is narrated in present tense by the three main characters involved in a love triangle—Elizabeth Schoenhof, Nate Schoenhof, and Lesje Green. Elizabeth and Nate's marriage decomposes (as the nature motifs in the novel parallel) while an affair blossoms between Nate and Lesje. As we often find in Atwood, the realistic conventions of the novel mask mythic elements and qualities *unlike* realistic fiction—"the exaggerated references to temporality, the minimal plot, and the dated narrative blocks that suggest scientific observers" (Stein, 1999, p. 70).

ENTRY POINT

A fairy tale and a classic movie, *The Wizard of Oz* can serve as an excellent entry point for *Life Before Man* as it mixes realism and mythic subtexts in ways similar to Atwood's novel. Also, Stein (1999) notes that critics have recognized that "each character lacks important parts and repairs the loss through a quest journey" (p. 66). Ultimately, the movie allows a classroom discussion of realism and fantasy, of linear depictions of reality and mythic truths.

Stein notes that *Life Before Man* is "Atwood's least-discussed novel" (p. 66), but it remains a valuable work for our classrooms. Let's look briefly at some of the elements of the novel we can address in our classes:

- The novel juxtaposes "the gray world of the city and the green world of nature" (Stein, 1999, pp. 65–66), a motif that recurs in the other three novels in this chapter. Atwood forces readers to consider the tension between city and rural life, a relevant issue for students. Here, the garden motif is less pronounced than in the three novels to be discussed later, but the implication is significant.

- As noted earlier, this novel allows a classroom exploration of realistic fiction and conventions. Further, Atwood's use of and manipulation of Realistic conventions are intertwined with her "recurring critique of Western science and its rational, linear worldview" (Stein, 1999, p. 68). We can add that the "novel's narrative structure turns the characters into spectacle, or scientific subjects," raising questions about objectivity in fiction and in science (Stein, p. 68).

CONNECTION

Stein (1999) identifies a parallel between *Life Before Man* and Eliot's *Middlemarch*. Atwood, Stein adds, herself claims that this novel is a homage to Eliot's work. These works can be paired to explore genre, the novel form, and many shared themes, such as "both argue against scientific determinism" (Stein, p. 66).

- With three narrators, the novel animates three views of reality, folding into her questioning of the value of objectivity—or even the value of pursuing objectivity. This layered approach to revealing reality is common and effective in Atwood, a motif that returns in *The Handmaid's Tale*.

- The title itself, *Life Before Man,* allows for many interpretations. Does it suggest a prehistoric motif (especially with a paleontologist main character)? Does it suggest a feminist motif, literally referring to males? Or does it connote some evolutionary statement about the development of humans? (Stein, 1999, p. 66).
- Mythological patterns course beneath the realistic veneer of this novel, as they do in most of Atwood's works. Mythic considerations of death and rebirth are interwoven with natural imagery and seasonal motifs "that may portend a more optimistic vision" than many see in the work (Stein, 1999, p. 66).
- Related to the scientific elements in the novel are "[m]otifs of seeing and being seen" (Stein, 1999, p. 68). These motifs are a powerful element in her consideration of objectivity and science (along with realism), but they also carry a feminist concern that intensifies by the publication of *The Handmaid's Tale.*
- The novel, according to Stein (1999), "reveals the limits of living according to clock time rather than event time or seasonal time" (p. 69). The dated text and numerous references to time contribute to Atwood's parody of realism and her thematic concerns about the regimented life lived by the clock.

ENTRY POINT

A classic and provocative parable, "Give It Up!," is one of Franz Kafka's jewels. In this brief scene where the narrator realizes his watch and the tower clock are out of sync, the narrator finds a policeman and asks for help, only to be told, "Give it up, give it up." This story of confused times and physical disorientation is a perfect entry point to the time motif in *Life Before Man;* Kafka's mix of genres and his tendency toward satire wrapped in a bleak setting prepare students for Atwood's similar qualities.

Life Before Man as a realistic novel with dystopian undertones leads naturally into *Bodily Harm,* a detective novel set in a dystopian Garden of Eden where we see Atwood's concern for politics increase and suggest her move to a futuristic dystopia in *The Handmaid's Tale.*

The Politics of Women's Bodies—*Bodily Harm*

"There wasn't as much to carry now that Jake wasn't there any more, which was just as well because the muscles in my left shoulder were aching," Rennie Wilford offers in the first paragraph of *Bodily Harm,* continuing, "I hadn't been keeping up the exercises" (p.

3). Reading as any mainstream novel might, these early words actually reveal the heavy elements that will prove this novel to be another dark story, another inverse Garden of Eden. Rennie's left shoulder hurts because she is recovering from a mastectomy, and she is also recovering from a break-up. This is a novel about the "politics of women's bodies" along with other issues of postcolonialism, governmental politics, and feminism (Stein, 1999, p. 71).

Set in the Caribbean, the novel recounts the escape Rennie Wilford seeks as she ventures to a paradise for a working vacation where she intends to write an article and recover her life, fragmented by her cancer and her lost relationship. By page 5, the reader finds a clue—literally a reference to the board game *Clue*—suggesting yet another manipulation of genre by Atwood; here, she "exploits the form of the detective thriller to parody and critique the genre" (Stein, 1999, p. 72). Yet, the novel ultimately is a political work, a harbinger of her more aggressively political *The Handmaid's Tale.*

ENTRY POINT

In a brilliant essay, "Laughter vs. Death," Margaret Atwood discusses issues at the center of her *Bodily Harm*—pornography and the meanings of such terms such as "pornography." Here, Atwood opens her discussion by explaining her own realization that she and a journalist meant two different things when using the term "pornography." This opening epiphany leads to a complex and revealing discussion of the meaning of words and the power of language, especially when people begin to consider censorship in free societies. Further, after clarifying that she sees erotica and pornography as different animals—one tame, the other rapacious—in *Writing with Intent,* Atwood (2005) offers "three other models for looking at 'pornography'" (p. 15). She ends the piece with an allusive question: "This leads us back to the key question: what is harm?" (p. 17)—making the essay an excellent entry point for the novel and simply a wonderful essential question for our students to ponder.

The personal politics and the wider governmental politics of the novel contribute to the unmasking of the Caribbean as an inverted Garden of Eden—a dystopia existing in the here and now, not in some future. Whether her dystopias are contemporary or futuristic, "Atwood changes the setting so as to exaggerate and expose some of the failings of our society, including disregard for the environment and the inequitable distribution of power between individuals" (Cooke, 2004, p. 113). Setting the ominous mood of the work, Atwood includes a quote from John Berger's *Ways of Seeing,* which harkens the powerlessness of women and establishes the power of a man's gaze, a motif included in *Life Before Man.*

As a foundational work for the futuristic *The Handmaid's Tale,* Atwood confronts the dark realities of paradise in *Bodily Harm* through continuing to wrestle with genre. We can use this novel as an opportunity for asking our students to experiment with genre in their own writing. That process includes asking students to discover and identify the conventions of a particular genre—such as the detective novel in *Bodily Harm* or Realism in *Life Before Man*—as a basis for writing both within and against those conventions. For students, this may work best as an assignment that looks closely at (while also attacking) the traditional analytical literary essay. According to the level of students in our classes, we can also ask them to attack conventions in surface features—grammar, mechanics, and usage. Using Atwood as a model, they should be encouraged to play with words as well.

CONNECTION

Another issue with genre can be addressed by pairing *Bodily Harm* with Atwood's book of poetry, *True Stories.* Stein (1999) connects the novel with the poetry collection as it has "strong thematic links to *Bodily Harm* that deals in part with political oppression and torture" (p. 71). Stein notes specifically "Notes Toward a Poem That Can Never Be Written"—which shares with the novel "political atrocities such as torture . . . and violence done to women" (p. 116). Of importance to our students in English courses is Atwood's own concern for "bearing witness to pain and violence" (Stein, p. 116). How and when do we raise our voices in the face of atrocities?

The politics of art is represented well by Atwood's *Bodily Harm.* As well, an effective way to frame what Atwood addresses in the novel is to begin with her "Amnesty International: An Address," included in *Second Words.* The speech offers yet another twist on genre; as a piece written to be spoken, this work provides an opportunity for students to consider the speech as a form. Yet, this speech also provides a foundational question that can guide a class discussion of her novel: "[W]hat is the writer's responsibility, if any, to the society in which he or she lives?" (Atwood, 1982, p. 393).

In the Amnesty International piece Atwood (1982) displays her precise and artful language well, offering a Disneyland analogy early in the speech that suggests the corrupt nature of all things American (here including a fictional "Pornoland" in her "Disneyland of the soul") and all things popular (p. 393). As she does in her novel and poetry collection, this speech briefly raises issues related to rugged individualism, politics, writers as witnesses, artistic freedom, the marketplace and art, and the interplay between power and silence. By the end of the speech, Atwood reveals her gift for the apt aphorism, a device crucial to the effective speech: "Freedom that exists as a result of the servitude of others is not true freedom," and "The most lethal weapon in the world's arsenals is not the neutron bomb or chemical warfare; but the human mind that devises such things and puts them to use" (p. 396).

With the speech providing a lens and with students working to take the opportunities to consider and reconsider genre conventions, *Bodily Harm* presents a number of avenues for us to pursue as a novel unit.

- Students need to consider colonialism and postcolonialism as historical contexts for this novel. For contemporary students, these facts of history as they pertain to the issues of power and oppression may seem *merely academic.* Novels dealing with these issues can help put life into ideas, can help bring something that appears a thing of the past to the here and now.

CONNECTIONS

Popular and critically acclaimed novels that address colonialism/postcolonialism along with issues of power and gender are Barbara Kingsolver's *The Poisonwood Bible* and Alice Walker's *The Color Purple.* These two works and Atwood's *Bodily Harm* require a knowledge of colonialism and the lingering impact of those practices on cultures and peoples throughout the world. The political dynamics at the government level along with the political dynamics of individuals play key roles in these novels—notably as power impacts the lives of women.

- Another concern in this novel is the workings of government, both as a process and as a subtle manipulation. While students may feel that the political violence in the novel is removed from their lives, we can stress Atwood's suggestion that politics and government can manipulate in many ways.
- The main character's cancer and mastectomy, according to Stein (1999), "become a metaphor for the disorder of the body politic" (p. 72). Again typical of Atwood is to offer in her book dedication a key political message; this novel is in part dedicated to Jennifer Rankin, an Australian poet who died of breast cancer. While Atwood implements sickness motifs in the novel as poetic device, she also addresses the impact of illness on women just as

she highlights the impact of political upheaval and corruption on women.

- Is this novel a detective novel? Here we have an interesting and rare look at genre fiction in our English classes that tends to marginalize any forms other than serious fiction—that fiction that cannot be classified as "genre." The novel itself mentions the board game Clue as part of Atwood's use and manipulation of the detective form.

- Motifs that support this novel include hand imagery, time motifs, disease and sickness metaphors, motifs confronting the contrast between surface and substance, dynamics mixing sex and violence, pornography, and motifs of food, hunger, and politics (Stein, 1999).

- The inverse Garden of Eden that is the Caribbean of the novel relies heavily on the drug culture. Again, political in nature, Atwood forces the reader to consider the culpability of the Western world, notably the U.S., in the drug world.

- The rape of the character Lora stands as a clear parallel to similar scenes concerning rape in Atwood's *The Handmaid's Tale.* Stein (1999) believes Rennie's "[r]eaching out to the wounded Lora" also allows Rennie to be "reborn" (p. 77).

CONNECTION

Atwood's short story "Rape Fantasies" is a brilliant work of narration and a perfect example of Atwood's ability to disturb the reader with her topics, her tone, and her deft use of ambiguity. The story is narrated from the perspective of a woman on a blind date—and possibly her impending rape by her date. The story explores the rise in interest in the 1970s of date rape; the work is chilling and well crafted. The tone of the narrator, who is attempting to talk her way out of being raped, leaves the reader fearful and somewhat unsure of what exactly is happening—as the narrator could be afraid for no real reason. Further, the story explores the concept of women considering rape as a sexual (and positive) fantasy. Atwood offers a wonderful unwrapping of that concept in having her narrator deconstruct the absurdity of rape fantasies as she talks to her date (rapist?).

- A final and key element of Atwood's novels is that "her protagonists become witnesses rather than activists" (Stein, 1999, p. 77). Rennie, as Offred/June in *The Handmaid's Tale,* is the messenger, the storyteller. For our students, this can lead to a wonderful discussion of the nature of action and the power of words.

Fulfilling a motif of the novel, the work ends with "She will never be rescued. She has already been rescued. She is not exempt. Instead, she is lucky" (p. 291). This same shifting—never be rescued to already been rescued—and the concept of "luck" are to be brought back to life in the more haunting and futuristic *The Handmaid's Tale.*

Atwood's Immodest Proposal— *The Handmaid's Tale*

In my twenty-plus years of teaching literature, few works can rival the teaching of *The Handmaid's Tale* in terms of its power as a work of fiction (*Invisible Man* by Ralph Ellison comes close here) and as a work read and loved by my students (*A Prayer for Owen Meany* by John Irving comes close). In her dedications and opening quotes, Atwood sets this futuristic dystopia in motion: the book is dedicated to Mary Webster (survivor of a hanging during the Salem witch trials) and Perry Miller (a Harvard professor who may be the model for James Darcy Pieixoto in the Historical Notes); and the three opening quotes are from the book of Genesis (thus, handmaid's), Swift's *A Modest Proposal,* and a Sufi proverb that may suggest better than anything the nature of Atwood's most famous work as both highly detailed and deeply ambiguous.

As noted earlier in this chapter, a perfect piece to open a unit on this novel is Atwood's "Writing Utopia," from *Writing with Intent* (as well as Vonnegut's "Science Fiction"). While *The Handmaid's Tale* suits our concerns for genre, I believe its larger value in the English classroom is Atwood's word play throughout blended into the narrative of the main character Offred (so named as a play on "Mrs."—the handmaid's name has the possessive "of" attached to the first name of the Commander), who appears to have been named June before this new society is formed. Word play runs throughout Offred's narration and supports many of the themes running throughout the novel—notably, as Cooke (2004) suggests, "the fallibility and limitations of narrative" (p. 125).

In the final chapter, "Historical Notes on *The Handmaid's Tale,*" the reader learns that the text of the entire novel is actually the transcription by academics of audio recordings made by Offred/June after her apparent escape from Gilead. Here is an ideal opportunity for students to discuss and explore perspective and multiple layers of story and narrative. In our daily lives, journalists record, transcribe and report, and we as readers are confronted with multiple layers of reality; a similar dynamic exists in the visual media. Students should be asked to peel back these layers and look closely at "truth" (the facts) and "Truth" (the enduring themes of human existence—if such exists).

Further, we discover that the academic setting of the conference in the Historical Notes and the transcription of the audio recordings are both deeply influenced by male perspectives and male biases, although the final chapter is set in 2195 (about 200 years past the main setting of Offred/June's experiences).

CONNECTIONS

In *Writing with Intent*, Atwood includes "George Orwell: Some Personal Connections"; this essay reveals Atwood's early interest in Orwell and his themes. She recalls reading *Animal Farm* at nine: "The pigs browbeat the others with ideology, then twist that ideology to suit their own purposes: their language games were evident to me even at that age" (p. 288). Later, Atwood identifies with *1984*—"probably because Winston Smith was more like me," as she compares the work to Aldous Huxley's *Brave New World* (p. 289). By the end of the essay, Atwood places *The Handmaid's Tale* in the context of her affinity for Orwell; then she places her novel in the context of a post-9/11 world: "Now it appears we face the prospect of two contradictory dystopias at once—open markets, closed minds" (p. 292). This essay can serve as a perfect literary connection to Orwell's works as well as a connection to the brave new world we have been facing since 9/11.

Book-length studies of this novel have been published so I see no need to attempt to create an exhaustive list of what we can do with this work in our English classes. However, I will touch on several wonderful discussions, lessons, and assignments that can grow from Atwood's most-taught novel. One powerful aspect of the novel is that Atwood has stated that every single event of this terrifying futuristic world has already happened in human history; she has compiled those horrors into her political and religious dystopia. Thus, the novel is a fictional history lesson both in the details of our history and in its commentary on history: As Atwood shows, whoever has power also has the words to tell history, thus shaping our perception of the truth about history.

CONNECTION

Howard Zinn has secured his place in popular culture as a historian of those who lost wars, those who previously had no voice. His *People's History of the United States* was mentioned by Will Hunting (Matt Damon) in *Good Will Hunting*, but his popularity among alternative and progressive thinkers was probably already guaranteed. For students, Zinn offers them a fresh perspective concerning the nature of history as it is impacted by those who write history. The historical aspects of *The Handmaid's Tale* are greatly supported if students begin to reconsider their perceptions of history—especially their trust that the history in their textbooks is objective.

When Atwood writes about Orwell, she argues that he—and by implication, she—is far more optimistic about the human condition than people are apt to note. For me, the most moving aspect of her novel is the human will that runs throughout. Offred/June recalls and clings to the things that have made her most human—even though some of those things have not been the best for her—such as her human relationships with her mother, her husband, and her lost daughter. The humanity of being connected to other humans is a profound argument of this novel, and it is a topic of value to our students. What is the state of the human condition?—the novel asks. And how far can the human spirit be pushed before it breaks? These and other questions about Offred/June in the most repressed conditions bubble up throughout her narrative.

Anther aspect of the novel that I believe is as important in the early twenty-first century as at any other point in history is highlighted by Atwood in her essay on George Orwell. Since 9/11, many people in free societies seem more willing to abdicate their freedoms in an effort to save their free government. This contradiction is given life in *The Handmaid's Tale*. In section five, Offred/June quotes Aunt Lydia as speaking about freedom while she and other women are in the Red Center: "There is more than one kind of freedom. . . . Freedom to and freedom from" (p. 24). In the previous society, the leaders of Gilead argue, "freedom to" destroyed humanity; in the new Republic, the theocracy offers the citizens "freedom from." Here is an excellent point for discussion among students. Atwood directly portrays the central distinction between progressive and conservative thought, particularly as it manifests itself in the early 2000s of the United States, particularly in the politics of right-wing conservatives. "We were a society dying . . . of too much choice," Aunt Lydia tells the handmaids—echoing the sentiment of the religious right in the U.S. in the early twenty-first century (p. 24).

Just as Atwood dramatizes the manipulation of words and ideology in her dystopia—inspired, it appears, by her reading Orwell—she also characterizes Offred/June as a woman who relishes words as part of her attempt to cling to her Self and her life. Wordplay is evident with the main character's name, "Offred." The practice of placing "of" before the commander's first name creates "off red" for the main character, a handmaid dressed in all red, a handmaid who turns out to be rebellious in her retelling of her tale (but not rebellious in her actions as Moira is). Again, I can't be exhaustive here, but let's look at some of the other wordplay in the novel:

- In part two, Offred/June plays with the lack of "sororize" as a female equal to fraternize. This concern for the sexism of language, thus power, runs throughout Offred/June's musings.
- When she thinks of her red outfit, she considers the word "habit," both a nun's cloak and "[h]abits are hard to break" (p. 24).
- Section seven begins with Offred/June thinking of the lie/lay distinction—a favorite of the oppressive English classroom! Here, Atwood raises the issues of passivity and action along with the sexual nature of language, including the sexist and aggressive nature of men's language toward women as sexual objects.
- As in "Rape Fantasies," Offred/June shares a flashback to her life before Gilead when she and Moira discuss date rape; as in her short story, their talk is mixed with humor that seems to make light of a serious issue (p. 38).
- When Offred/June discovers the secret word of the underground, "Mayday," she associates it with its homophone *"m'aidez,"* French for "help me" (pp. 43–44).
- While visiting the doctor, Offred/June discusses the use of the word "sterile," "a forbidden word" in Gilead: "There is no such thing as a sterile man anymore, not officially" (p. 61). This raises the issue of taboo language and the power a government has when it chooses "official" reality for its citizens.
- During the Ceremony—the once-a-month copulation between handmaid and Commander—Offred/June contemplates the proper language for the act itself, confronting the reader with the language we use for sex.
- Words appear as stitching on a small pillow—of faith, hope, and charity, only the pillow with "faith" remains.
- Moira acts: "Moira had power now, she'd been set loose, she'd set herself loose. She was now a loose woman" (p. 133).
- The illicit activity that Offred/June and the Commander enjoy is playing Scrabble—a word game. She notes that it is something the Commander and Serena Joy cannot do (since women are denied language) so "[n]ow it's desirable" (p. 139). Later, Offred/June thinks, "Caught in the act, sinfully Scrabbling. Quick, eat those words" (p. 181).
- When Offred/June discusses Moira's homosexuality, her language is revealing: "[S]ince she'd decided to prefer women" (p. 172). The use of "decided" is loaded with implications about

Offred/June's perception of sexuality as a choice.

- When thinking of her life before Gilead, Offred/June plays with the word "job," ending with "The Book of Job." Here, the reader learns of the overthrow of the previous government, noting the initial blaming of the events on Islamic fanatics (an eerie reference for a mid-1980s novel).

- Throughout the novel, Atwood alludes to Freudian terminology; in section twenty-nine, Offred/June plays with "penis envy" in the form of "Pen Is Envy" (p. 186).

- Late in the novel "*Aunt Lydia sucks*" stands as a key act of rebellion, raising issues of taboo language and the sexuality of language as dehumanizing of women (p. 222).

- In section forty-two, Offred/June acknowledges the use of "girls" instead of "ladies" when referring to the handmaids; the Wives are called "ladies" (p. 274).

The word motif running through the novel lends itself to our English classes as does the postmodern consideration of reconstructing reality through storytelling. Offred/June often tells one version of events only to stop and reconsider and even retell the events. For our students, this novel raises a question about perspective and reality. Offred/June's narration is filled with tellings and retellings, dreams, and flashbacks. Stein (1999) explains "the multilayering of texts brings into question the conventions of storytelling, literary criticism, and interpretation" (p. 79).

CONNECTION

In Virginia Woolf's *A Room of One's Own,* she says, "All I could do was to offer you an opinion upon one minor point—a woman must have money and a room of her own if she is to write fiction, and that, as you will see, leaves the great problem of the true nature of woman and the true nature of fiction unsolved" (p. 2). Stein (1999) believes Atwood is alluding to Woolf's work because Atwood places Offred/June in a room alone, thinking, musing, and telling her story.

Atwood's argument that her work is *not* science fiction grows from her use of satire. In other words, Atwood's novel is set in the future, but it speaks directly about the world contemporary to Atwood as she wrote the novel—notably the rising religious-conservative nature of politics in the United States. The Moral Majority and the election of Ronald Reagan represented for Atwood a serious danger to the freedom she cherishes. The novel, then, serves as a parody of the Religious Right. That parody includes the following:

- The Republic of Gilead answers the question, What would a biblically based government look like? The answer is, of course, horrifying. Yet, every central aspect of Gilead is directly drawn from the text of the Bible.
- The Commander's wife, Serena Joy, appears to be based on infamous televangelist Tammy Faye Baker (Cooke, 2004) with a possible nod to right-wing icon Phyllis Schlafly (Stein, 1999). This character addresses the irony Atwood sees in women supporting sexist ideology couched as religious doctrine.
- The patriarchal hierarchy of the society is also biblical and parallels the paradigms that continue to dominate modern society. Atwood's Historical Notes, set in 2195, appears to argue that society and academia remain sexist well into the future.
- The rituals of the society, such as the Ceremony and the Prayvaganza, represent the corruption of religious ceremony.

While some may find the work offensive because of the satire, it is clear that Atwood's parody is aimed at misguided religion—not religion as a pure practice. A better explanation of the focus of Atwood's satire is the *corruption* of religious ideology for patently irreligious purposes—again spurred, it seems, by Atwood's reading of Orwell.

For students in the twenty-first century, students who have grown up in the wake of 9/11, *The Handmaid's Tale* may ultimately be a work best suited to confront the dangers of fundamentalism. The dystopia Atwood creates is not unlike the world we face today. In a "Note to the Reader," Atwood warns: "History proves that what we have been in the past we could be again" (p. 316).

Atwood's Slippery Slope—*Oryx and Crake*

If Atwood is skilled at anything, she is adept at making her readers uncomfortable. In the Historical Notes of *The Handmaid's Tale,* we discover that by 2195 the world has become the toxic wasteland some warn of us today; the racial balance of North America has shifted greatly; disease has ravaged fertility, and humanity's love affair with war toys and chemicals has ravaged whatever disease has not (p. 304). Less than a decade passed, and Atwood (2005) found herself called to write a novel she had not anticipated, as explained in "Writing *Oryx and Crake*" from *Writing with Intent:* "[I]t was while looking over Philip's balcony at the red-necked crakes scuttling about in the underbrush that *Oryx and Crake* appeared to me, almost in its entirety" (p. 284). She continues by explaining this dystopian novel is yet another *"what if"* book (p. 285).

This explanatory essay offers a great deal of insight into both the novel and why we should bring it into our classes. Briefly, here, we will discuss *Oryx and Crake* as the anchoring work in a novel unit addressing the environment and humanity's obsessions with war and technology—to the detriment of humanity. Atwood (2005) explains in "Writing *Oryx and Crake*" (available as the "Perfect Storms" link on the *Oryx and Crake* webpage) that she began the novel before 9/11, and then had that drafting interrupted by serendipity: "It's deeply unsettling when you're writing about a fictional catastrophe and then a real one happens" (p. 285). The essay reveals both Atwood the writer and Atwood the scientist; her brain clearly functions in both paradigms. Further, she offers yet again an argument that this novel is "speculative fiction, not a science fiction proper" (p. 285). It is, however, as she phrases it, a *what if* novel: "The *what if* of *Oryx and Crake* is simply, *What if we continue down the road we're already on? How slippery is the slope? What are our saving graces? Who's got the will to stop us?*" (pp. 285–286).

- -

ENTRY POINT

Atwood joins an impressive list of writers who seek to warn humanity of our follies. Kurt Vonnegut suffers a similar burden to Atwood in that he is often marginalized as a science fiction writer. His canon is certainly filled with an impressive array of dystopian works. Recently, Vonnegut has turned to making more direct commentaries on the environment and on humanity's disregard for planet Earth. His *A Man without a Country* includes a number of essays that would be excellent entry points for Atwood's *Oryx and Crake.* Vonnegut (2005), in that volume, declares: "Don't spoil the party, but here's the truth: We have squandered our planet's resources, including air and water, as though there were no tomorrow, so now there isn't going to be one" (pp. 44–45).

- -

Oryx and Crake offers many opportunities as a novel unit or as a source for studying the environment and humanity's apparent disregard for the planet. Additionally, the novel has a wonderful companion website (www.oryxandcrake.com) referenced in the "Acknowledgements," along with many connections for studying the novel. The website and the "Acknowledgements" suggest several ways to approach the novel:

- Atwood herself links her novel with other works. Virginia Woolf's *To the Lighthouse,* Anne Carson's *The Beauty of the Husband,* Samuel Beckett's *Mercier and Camier*—all are noted in the "Acknowledgements."
- Quotes on refrigerator magnets are throughout the novel and noted on the webpage under "Related Links," then "Fridge Magnets."

The quotes are interesting and both allusive and illusive, such as "Little spoat/gider, who made thee?" which mangles a line from William Blake using the lab-created animals of the future.

- The "Acknowledgements" also refer to animal intelligence experiments, which may be a fruitful source of research for students.
- Finally, Atwood acknowledges "magazines and newspapers and non-fiction science writers encountered over the years" for her sources in a novel (p. 367). Here, we might ask students to create and write their own fiction from a nonfiction source.

CONNECTIONS

As a work concerning the environment, as a warning to preserve the environment, we could place *Oryx and Crake* in a unit on the environment as a topic within the U.S. tradition where literary and academic (and scientific) forces clash with popular perceptions. A grounding work to connect is Henry David Thoreau's *Walden*, which in many ways is a seminal environmental treatise in American literature. A perfect companion to these two works is *An Inconvenient Truth*, the documentary concerning former Vice President Al Gore's attempt to spread the word about global warming. The video helps place Atwood's novel and Thoreau's classic in a political context since the public debate over global warming (and about many issues in science, such as evolutionary biology) has remained highly polarized and deeply flawed among political ideologues.

The novel's webpage (available in several versions in different countries) offers an excerpt of the novel, an audio reading of an excerpt, and a reading guide for students. As a futuristic work, the web-based approach might be even more appealing to students entering our classes, but it also allows us to use this novel to discuss the pros and cons of technology while actually interacting with that technology. A number of essential questions can flow from reading the novel and interacting with the webpage: Have computers and the Internet eroded or enhanced literacy among people? What are the social and economic implications of people's access to technology? Does Atwood's work address technology favorably or unfavorably? Are the disasters in the novel the result of technology or flaws in humanity?

Finally, we can approach *Oryx and Crake* both as an extension of many of Atwood's favorite themes and motifs and as unlike her other works. First, this novel is similar to *The Handmaid's Tale* as a futuristic dystopia and as an artistic commentary on gender, power, humanity's weaknesses, sex and violence (pornography), government, and perspective. Yet, this novel is the lone work narrated completely from the point of view of a male character. The limited omniscient narration concerning the marooned Snowman feels similar to the story told by Offred/June, but the third-person point of view and the male perspective give this novel a quality we cannot find in other Atwood works. Here, she challenges her readers to consider the future as a world of Man—not unlike the misogynistic tone of the Historical Notes in *The Handmaid's Tale,* the world of Snowman is a lone man's world. And this lone man watches the end of the world as we know it unfold in the most disturbing ways, including his own love for Oryx—a child found by Snowman/Jimmy in exploitive pornography.

In Chapter Five, we move on to the later novels by Atwood, brilliant and experimental works. Later, we will explore her short fiction, her poetry, and her expanding canon of other works, including children's literature. For this chapter, we leave as *Oryx and Crake* ends: "Zero hour, Snowman thinks. Time to go" (p. 374).

ENTRY POINTS AND CONNECTIONS

"Science Fiction," Kurt Vonnegut, *Wampeters, Foma & Granfalloons*

"Writing Utopia," Margaret Atwood, *Writing with Intent*

The Wizard of Oz, L. Frank Baum

Middlemarch, George Eliot

"Give It Up!," Franz Kafka, *The Basic Kafka*

"Laughter vs. Death," Margaret Atwood, *Writing with Intent*

True Stories, Margaret Atwood

The Poisonwood Bible, Barbara Kingsolver

The Color Purple, Alice Walker

"Rape Fantasies," Margaret Atwood

"George Orwell: Some Personal Connections," Margaret Atwood, *Writing with Intent*

1984 and *Animal Farm,* George Orwell

People's History of the United States, Howard Zinn

A Room of One's Own, Virginia Woolf

A Man without a Country, Kurt Vonnegut

Walden, Henry David Thoreau

An Inconvenient Truth, Davis Guggenheim, dir. (Al Gore)

Chapter Five

Later Novels

Mythologies of and for Women

Writers with catalogues of works as long and diverse as Atwood's are rarely as able as Atwood is to return again and again to motifs and themes while re-visioning those patterns with the sort of clarity and complexity that Atwood achieves. After the larger acclaim she received for *The Handmaid's Tale,* Atwood clearly remained driven as a writer, broadly, and as a novelist who would offer a wonderful collection of later novels (so far) that are ideal for our classrooms. Except for *Oryx and Crake,* which we already discussed with her dystopian works, we will explore her novels after and including *Cat's Eye* (1998), works that in many ways are novels about storytelling and myth making, both of and for women.

Atwood continues to work within and to manipulate genres in her later works—*Cat's Eye, The Robber Bride, Alias Grace, The Blind Assassin,* and *The Penelopiad.* As well, these works are considerations of female relationships/friendships, the woman as artist, and the balance of power between oppressors and their victims. Images of water and mirrors, motifs of "doubles and doubling," mythic patterns, and "questions of identity and interpretation" recur throughout Atwood's stories that offer her continued interest in the nature of storytelling and the importance of perspective in those stories.

Portrait of the Female Artist at Middle Age— *Cat's Eye* as Retelling

In Chapter Three, I looked at *Lady Oracle* as a novel addressing a woman as an artist; *Cat's Eye* returns to this concern more than a decade later. Elaine Risley is a successful fifty-year-old visual artist who is returning to Toronto for a retrospective of her works. Her return is paralleled in this story told as a "fictionalized autobiography" (Stein, 1999, p. 87) through Elaine's recalling her traumatic childhood that includes a haunting episode when she falls into a ravine and a problematic relationship with Cordelia. Thematically rich, this novel is driven by allusion and by Atwood's ability to layer narrative with theoretical considerations—about the nature of time and the nature of truth within storytelling.

ENTRY POINT

Similar to her use of mirrors (and water imagery) in *Lady Oracle* in "Tricks with Mirrors," Atwood "empowers the mirror, . . . giving it a voice" (Cooke, 2004, p. 98). In the poem, the speaker becomes a mirror and taunts her reader/audience: "Mirrors/are the perfect lovers" (11. 4–5). A student discussion of the mirror imagery and the voice of the poem fits perfectly with an exploration of those elements in the novel. The poem ends by shifting the metaphor to "a door" and then "a pool," acknowledging the references directly as metaphors, and challenging the reader as Atwood often does.

CONNECTION

Critics (Cooke, 2004; Stein, 1999) recognize Atwood's use of allusion that reinforces her interest in the patterns of myth and her manipulation of classic forms. Through Atwood's naming Elaine's friend Cordelia, the novel builds on the allusion to King Lear's daughter. As well, Cooke notes the use of Burnham High School, another Shakespearean reference (to the woods near Macbeth's castle). For students, we can ask how these allusions reinforce the characterization of Cordelia and how the allusions contribute to Atwood's motifs and themes. Since critics are quick to note and explore these allusions in Atwood (as much critical material we have in our schools is heavily driven by New Criticism), we can have students research what critics suggest about these allusions in order to explore the assumptions of traditional literary criticism.

"Time is not a line but a dimension," opens the novel, "like the dimensions of space" (p. 3). The novel begins with the word "time," following Atwood including a Stephen Hawking passage to preface the novel. (She names Elaine's brother "Stephen" as well.) Blended with the narrative, then, is Atwood contemplating the nature of time, particularly as it is related to the retelling of a story—such as the story of Elaine's childhood told as a flashback during her retrospective art show. Atwood has wrestled with these concepts before; *The Handmaid's Tale* reveals to the reader at the end that that "tale" is a recreation of several layers (an audio tape transcribed and given form, importantly, by male academics). In *Cat's Eye,* the story is in the hands of the main character herself, Elaine, who has found her voice through her art and in the face of her own powerlessness as a child within the world of female friendships.

Stein (1999) and Cooke (2004) recognize that this novel pushes male characters farther into the background and dramatizes many levels of relationships among women (and girls) as friends. Cooke sees the novel as both a *bildungsroman* (coming-of-age novel, such as *Portrait of the Artist as a Young Man*) and a *kunstlerroman* (a novel of the rise of an artist, also found in Joyce's novel). Elaine as a child seems unaware of how friendships among girls function since her life has been sheltered by her father's work and her close relationship with her brother. The novel raises issues about childhood dynamics that should prove interesting to our students—issues of how friendships form, how power functions in those friendships, how cliques form, how and why children ostracize other children, and how children often form underground cultures out of sight of adults as a way to acquire power.

CONNECTION

Patricia Hersch's *A Tribe Apart* is a fascinating case study of teenage culture, as shown through the eyes of young people brought to light by Hersch. This nonfiction work is thought provoking in its analogy that children and teens live in a "tribe apart" from adults. My college students find this work readable and fascinating—some feeling she is perceptive and others leery of her stories and conclusions. Regardless, this book offers a well-written nonfiction companion work to *Cat's Eye* as explorations of friendship and childhood/teen subcultures.

Cat's Eye is a long and complex work that deals with far more than contemplations of time and storytelling, with friendships among women, and with the role of women artists in the patriarchal art world. For our classrooms, we can also ask students to explore the following:

- The cat's eye marble from Elaine's childhood lends the novel its title and a motif throughout the novel. How does that image work in the novel?

- As a fictional autobiography, how does knowledge of Atwood's own biography (Stein, 1999, p. 87) help the reader understand the work?

- Elaine and Cordelia share a complex and troubling relationship throughout the novel; how are the two characters connected, and how does their relationship evolve throughout the work? What does the characterization of their relationship contribute to the novel's major themes? (Consider Atwood's use of mirrors and mirror images [Cooke, 2004, p. 108].)

- Along with the quote from Stephen Hawking, Atwood opens the novel with a quote about a severed head from Eduardo Galeano. If the Hawking quote reinforces Atwood's theme about time, what does the Galeano passage contribute to the novel?

- Critics (Stein, 1999; Cooke, 2004) recognize throughout Atwood's work an interest in a feminist perspective of the gaze—typically noted as a predatory act by men who objectify women. The cat's eye motif is literally a marble, but the novel does address staring and eye images throughout the work. How does Atwood reframe the power of the gaze in the relationships of women in this novel?

- Stein (1999) discusses Atwood's use of "figuring and disfiguring, facing and defacing" in the novel (pp. 90–91). How do these motifs manifest themselves in the novel, and how do they contribute to the novel's larger themes?

Two final larger ways to implement this novel in our classes include autobiography and the use of fairy tales, both of which can be significant units during the study of *Cat's Eye.* Since the novel shows Elaine recalling and unraveling her traumatic childhood, we can ask students to consider their own pasts and to write memoir scenes as ways to reconsider their lives. I have addressed the value of having students write memoirs in the first volume of this series on Barbara Kingsolver (Thomas, 2005a). Briefly, I believe this activity allows them to focus on their writing craft since their content, their lives, is readily available to them. As a writing assignment with *Cat's Eye,* we can add Atwood's concern for the power of telling and retelling a life. A possible twist to memoir and autobiography could be asking students to form pairs in order to tell each other stories of their lives, which leads to their writing the lives they are told. Here, they would be forced to consider accuracy and truth as they are impacted by the writer's craft of narration.

One way Atwood infuses her novel with mythological patterns is her use of fairy tales—Grimms' "Rapunzel" and Hans Christian Andersen's "The Snow Queen." Stein believes that the two fairy tales inform the larger narrative of the novel: "In each story the oppressed youth regains freedom by learning sympathy, human feeling, and connection" (p. 92). Our students can be asked how these fairy tales and those themes support the story of Elaine and Cordelia. Further, as essentially a novel about relationships between and among women, students should explore how Atwood incorporates the motifs of fairy tales—patterns that are paternalistic and about princes saving maidens in distress—in a complex feminist work.

As a work of art, *Cat's Eye* explores the regenerative power of art—for Elaine, her paintings. Cooke (2004) explains Elaine's last painting: "What the Virgin and the marble she holds represent is Elaine's recovery of her memory of the dark time of her childhood and also of the value of seeing that darkness" (p. 112). In her *The Robber Bride,* characters face many versions of the same character's life story, motifs and themes seen before in *Lady Oracle* and *Cat's Eye* but brought to life in this 1993 work as an investigation of the femme fatale, Zenia.

From "Z" to "A"—*The Robber Bride* and the Art of Illusion

Stein (1999) explains that "*The Robber Bride* is a woman-centered book that . . . transforms the traditional Robber Bridegroom tale (an Atwood favorite) of the murderous husband into a woman's story" (p. 96). This work is well suited for the classroom since it is a rich source for students to explore classic tales and classic patterns as Atwood asks them to reconsider many of the assumptions (literary and cultural) that drive classic narratives.

CONNECTION

Eudora Welty's *The Robber Bridegroom,* published in 1942, provides an excellent companion work to Atwood's novel. Welty also incorporates and manipulates the Grimms's fairy tale while including other mythological patterns such as Cupid and Psyche. Welty and Atwood share many qualities and concerns as women writers, but they have different literary groundings, Welty as a Southerner and Atwood as a Canadian. Further, both writers often confront readers with peculiar gothic humor and dark elements that challenge expectations about narratives and storytelling.

Patterns and motifs found in tales and fables in several cultures suggest that humans share some of these patterns in our biology—an argument posed by Carl Jung. "Collective unconscious" and "archetype" are Jungian concepts often left to discussions in fields *other* than literature, but my students felt our exploration of these terms and Joseph Campbell's application of Jungian perspectives to religion helped them tremendously as readers of complex texts, particularly the large number of texts in literature that rely on mythic patterns and allusions.

Either before reading or while discussing Atwood's novel, students should do research on the following, as an exploration of Jungian concepts and the many ways in which mythological patterns emerge in the stories of different people:

- Both Jung's and Campbell's discussions of "archetype" and "collective unconscious" should be researched and clarified for our students. Often these terms are oversimplified and misrepresented, particularly for young people. Here, we should seek a complex and evolving understanding of these terms as they impact our students as readers and writers. One excellent source for this topic is Joseph Campbell's *The Power of Myth,* an interview conducted by Bill Moyers for PBS.
- The Grimms's *The Robber Bridegroom* fairy tale should be read (available on-line: http://www.pitt.edu/~dash/grimm040.html) and analyzed, both for the pattern that it provides other writers and for the cultural assumptions inherent in the tale about gender, marriage, and parent-child relationships.

ENTRY POINT

If we are concerned that our students will have little interest in Grimms's fairy tales, we do not have to look too far—Hollywood. In 2005, Terry Gilliam directed *The Brothers Grimm,* starring the popular Matt Damon and Heath Ledger. This movie would be an excellent entry point for exploring the classic fairy tales, specifically *The Robber Bridegroom.*

- Related tales, *The Robber's Bride* and *The Story of Mr. Fox,* should also be read and examined closely as they relate to *The Robber Bridegroom* (available on-line: http://www.pitt.edu/~dash/type0955.html#fox).
- Students could also read and discuss Roald Dahl's *Fantastic Mr. Fox* to compare his children's book of the tale with Atwood's and Welty's works.

- Possibly already familiar to students are the stories of *Bluebeard* (available on-line: http://www.pitt.edu/~dash/type0312.html).
- Finally, students could search for allusions to the tales in other works of literature; one notable allusion is in William Shakespeare's *Much Ado About Nothing* (1.1).

Ultimately, this research should lead, I believe, to helping students see how writers use mythological patterns, motifs, and allusions as tools to express the larger ideas in their works. *We must be careful to avoid making these searches for mythic patterns and allusions appear to be the goal of what readers do.* What students can learn is that skilled readers are sensitive to the complex messages writers create for them.

Of course, the real value of this novel is that readers are engaged by the wonderful gifts of Atwood, gifts that, for most readers, lie beneath the surface. The unbraiding that we do in our English classes is *not* how most readers function; in fact, most of us who are skilled and dedicated readers set our analysis aside when we read *for pleasure.* It is often in our best interest and in the best interest of students to allow discussions of the pleasure in reading Atwood to break our habits of critical analysis.

"The story of Zenia ought to begin when Zenia began," opens *The Robber Bride* (p. 3). Again, the introductory quotes to Atwood's fiction help the reader see where Atwood is going in her work: Oscar Wilde's "Illusion is the first of all pleasures" is one of three opening passages, and it suggests Atwood is dealing with illusion. That illusion appears to be Atwood's continuing interest in storytelling as this novel looks at Zenia through the eyes and stories of three characters—Antonia Freemont, called Tony; Charis; and Roz. As Stein (1999) points out, Atwood renames all of her characters while building Zenia's name from parts of the other three women who tell her story, linking the characters by the naming and renaming (p. 100).

As a novel about a feminine Robber Bride, Zenia as femme fatale, *The Robber Bride* explores each of the three storytellers' lives through their versions of Zenia. The stories reinforce an extended consideration of victimhood, a recurring topic in Atwood's works. Atwood herself has described Zenia as the "mirror image" of Shakespeare's Ophelia, "the pallid, pure woman, the quintessential victim" (Stein, 1999, p. 95). As I have discussed earlier, the novel shares with folktales a view of how victims overcome their victimizers; yet, in Atwood, the dynamic is among women who have used men in that power play.

Stein (1999) recognizes that this "novel explores and problematizes questions of identity, good and evil, heterosexual relationships, friendship, war, history, and victimization"—a hefty list (p. 96). But Stein also notes that the novel looks closest at storytelling; Atwood's copyright of the novel is attributed to O. W. Toad (a shuffling of the letters in "Atwood"), "signal[ing] the importance of wordplay in the novel" (p. 97). Let's focus here on how Atwood explores storytelling through wordplay in her four characters and their intertwined stories.

One significant element readers can anticipate in Atwood's novels is her use of structure through the titling of her chapters and sections. (This is a powerful motif in *The Handmaid's Tale,* for example.) In *The Robber Bride,* the story is framed by the first chapter, "Onset," followed by "The Toxique," which serves as the title for both the second and sixth chapters. The third, fourth, and fifth chapters are the stories of Zenia by the three main characters—"Black Enamel" (Tony), "Weasel Nights" (Charis), and "The Robber Bride" (Roz). The novel ends with "Outcome."

Tony is the narrative focus of the opening and last chapters; renamed, she is the focus of Atwood's thematic interest in history as a form of storytelling, thus biased by the historian/storyteller. In "Onset," readers are prepared for the major threads of the novel. As noted above, the novel begins by referencing the beginning of Zenia, whose name suggests "from 'z' to 'a,'" a reversal of order just as "history is written backward, after the fact, by the victors" (Stein, 1999, p. 97). We learn that Tony sees Zenia as a "puzzle, a knot," to be unraveled much as she explains history to her students: "History is a construct, she tells her students. Any point of entry is possible and all choices are arbitrary" (p. 4).

CONNECTION

The traditional modernist view of history and of the historian depends on a belief in and a pursuit of objectivity. Atwood often challenges these modernist views of history, art, storytelling, and science. Tony, as both historian and one of the storytellers in *The Robber Bride,* focuses the novel on challenging the traditional view of history as unbiased, although Tony is partial to wars since they have "clear outcomes" (p. 4). I suggested Howard Zinn's *People's History of the United States* in Chapter Four because Zinn is the most recognized and respected postmodern historian as he admits and embraces the inherent bias of being a historian. Zinn's memoir, *You Can't Be Neutral on a Moving Train,* is an ideal connection to Atwood's novel as Zinn narrates his life story while personifying his professional stance that all stories, including the story of history, is shaded by who chooses to tell that story. Readers learn about Zinn's life while watching the Civil Rights movement unfold around him.

Tony's role as historian and interest in war suggest "the theme of war is a central one in the novel" (Stein, 1999, p. 101). World War II has shaped the lives of these characters; further, many of the characters have their relationships expressed as war. One of the wordplays in the novel (which echoes the wordplay in *The Handmaid's Tale*)—"raw sexes war" (Atwood revels in palindromes)—reinforces that motif. Stein also suggests Zenia is a "symbolic embodiment of war," who is connected throughout the novel with several wars—Vietnam, the Gulf War, bombings in Lebanon (p. 101). Yet, as Tony realizes, "[H]istory is not a true palindrome. . . . We can't really run it backwards and end up at a clean start" (p. 109). And such is the case of the retellings of Zenia's life.

CONNECTION

A powerful image of Kurt Vonnegut's *Slaughterhouse-Five* is Billy Pilgrim's fascination with watching war film *backward*. Vonnegut's most well-known and celebrated novel looks backward and forward—and in directions we can't quite anticipate—at war and history in many ways we find in Atwood's *The Robber Bride*. Vonnegut, Atwood, and Zinn offer perspectives that confront modernist assumptions about valuing the view of the winners.

As a final point, we should have students return to Atwood's view of victims; in the novel, the three women who tell Zenia's stories, stories never told by Zenia herself, appear to gain power over their own lives when Zenia dies, for a second time, as the novel ends. The connection of storytelling and victimization appears to suggest a power to storytelling since "a new interpretation of the past . . . may release each of them from the old stories that keep them in victim positions" (Stein, 1999, p. 102). Issues of power, storytelling, and history come to life again in Atwood's next novel, *Alias Grace,* the novelization of an infamous murder in Canada.

The Gaps of Stories (Re)told—*Alias Grace* as Confrontation of the Historical Novel

Reminiscent of Nathaniel Hawthorne's opening scene in *The Scarlet Letter, Alias Grace* begins with Grace Marks imprisoned: "I've been shut up in here since the age of sixteen" (p. 5). Atwood's wordplay—"shut up"—suggests Grace's silence as well as her imprisonment; she adds, "[I]t's not easy being quiet and good, it's like hanging on to the edge of a bridge when you've already fallen over" (p. 5). Again, words with double meanings, "hanging," introduce the reader to a novel of multiple versions of reality, versions that all include different levels of silence, imprisonment, and the threat of execution.

Students asked to read *Alias Grace* will be faced with many of Atwood's thematic patterns; they need to be prepared to explore the historical novel in its traditional forms as well as Atwood's manipulation of those conventions. For our classrooms, an ideal entry into the novel is Atwood's own "In Search of *Alias Grace:* On Writing Canadian Historical Fiction," included in *Writing with Intent.* Let's begin with Atwood's essay before turning to the novel itself.

Although much of Atwood's "In Search" appears to be about the growth of Canadian literature, all students will gain from her insights about historical fiction in general, the nature of conventions in literature, the dynamics surrounding any country's body of literature, and her own odyssey as author of *Alias Grace* (or any novel). Her discussion begins with time: "Like all beings alive on Middle Earth, we're trapped by time and circumstance" (p. 159). This essay, as in *The Robber Bride* and *Alias Grace,* weaves an argument about both fiction and history being *subjective*—bound by the perspectives of those who choose to write and the times in which those writers live. Atwood makes no distinction between "real human beings" and "fictional characters" (p. 159).

Since anyone choosing to tell a story is bound by her or his perceptions, reality is at the mercy of that storyteller: "I remember this very clearly, so it must be true, and there's your individual memory," she explains about her memory of "build[ing] snow forts that were much bigger than the Parliament Buildings" (p. 160). The pursuit of objectivity, then, is fruitless—in fiction, autobiography, and history. From here, she turns to what those who narrate *should* pursue; that is, narrative is built on individuals, thus laying the "brick-by-brick, life-by-life, day-by-day foundations" of storytelling (p. 160).

The broad assertions offered by Atwood often resonate on both a large scale and a small scale. When she states, "As a rule, we tend to remember the awful things done to us and to forget the awful things we did," she offers historical examples such as the firebombing of Dresden (a perfect example of horrific forgotten history, forgotten by those who did the firebombing), but this statement fits perfectly into the central patterns of Grace Marks's story in the novel (p. 160). And, since Atwood has stated often that her novels are driven by *questions,* she adds, "Here is the conundrum, for history and individual memory alike, and therefore for fiction also: How do we *know* we know what we think we know?" (p. 161). With that, she returns in her discussion to the importance of time in all fiction and the nature of historical fiction in general.

In the twentieth century, she argues, Europeans have "been on the whole more interested in forgetting" (p. 162). For example, she notes the paintings of Salvador Dali and writings by Samuel Beckett and Milan Kundera—and their titles directly concerned with memory and forgetting. Now, she is asking her reader to see her discussion in the context of her grounding in both George Orwell (the Memory Hole of *1984*) and the problems posed by postmodern perspectives, especially for Canadian artists. Further, she frames her discussion in the context of traditional historical fiction, those works often assigned for students to read in school—Sir Walter Scott and James Fenimore Cooper, as *the* writers of the form; *Vanity Fair, Middlemarch, A Tale of Two Cities, Ivanhoe,* and *Treasure Island,* as *the* novels (p. 164).

Next, she may lose many readers and students with her discussion of the evolution of a consciousness about "Canadian literature," but I believe here is a crucial moment for us to address an issue we rarely confront in our English classes: How and why do some writers and some works gain value in any country? In school, we tend to hand students texts—whether it is literature or a history text—and expect everyone to embrace that text without any consideration for its value or its quality. Texts taught in schools are authoritative by the nature of their being assigned; students (and teachers) are expected to treat them with respect quite passively. As a writer—and as an adult—Atwood confesses that she learned to question texts and objectivity late in her life, at least later than during her formal schooling as a young person. We should not allow such thoughtlessness with our students.

Before she turns to her writing of *Alias Grace,* Atwood discusses her own experience with American Literature, noting *Moby-Dick,* Walt Whitman, and Hawthorne's *The Scarlet Letter.* For Atwood, the historical fiction written in any time, by any people, and about any time is for far more than capturing that past through fiction: "[B]y taking a long, hard look backward, we place ourselves" (p. 170).

CONNECTIONS

Two classic works of American literature, one of mid-nineteenth century and one of mid-twentieth century, take "long, hard look[s] backward" to the Puritan era in the United States (formed in the seventeenth century, of course)—*The Scarlet Letter,* by Nathaniel Hawthorne, and *The Crucible,* by Arthur Miller. Both works pair well with each other, because of their use of Puritan settings, and both works connect well with *Alias Grace* since all three concern the guilt or innocence of women caught in sin and crime while facing cultures and judicial systems flawed by human perspective. If Hawthorne and Miller are looking back at the flaws in Puritan society, if Atwood is peeling back the layers of truth and untruth surrounding the trial of Grace Marks, they are all three also holding a magnifying glass up to the times in which we live: "You want squalor, lies, and corruption? Hell, we've got 'em homegrown, and not only that, we always have had, and there's where the past comes in," Atwood explains ("In Search," p. 168).

The last several pages of Atwood's consideration of historical fiction tell the story of Atwood coming to write *Alias Grace*—the story of a story of a multi-layered story. The genesis of this novel is traced to Atwood writing a book of poetry, *The Journals of Susanna Moody,* in the mid-1960s about Susanna Moody. The writings of Moody included the story of Grace Marks, whom Moody met in 1851 and wrote about in *Life in the Clearings.* While this distant beginning for the novel is interesting in itself, what also stands out is Atwood's development as a critical thinker: "That was the first version of the story [Grace's story] I came across, and being young, and still believing that 'nonfiction' meant 'true,' I did not question it" (p. 171). *This* is something our students need to consider—both Atwood's revelation about nonfiction and truth along with their own assumptions concerning nonfiction and truth. This essay allows us to continue to confront our students' knowledge of and assumptions about genre as well as their evolving perceptions of truth, Truth, and the objectivity/subjectivity debates.

The Moody project turned into another version for TV and a dropped attempt at the stage, but Atwood explains that in the early 1990s "[a] scene came to me vividly," and that was to be the novel *Alias Grace* (p. 172). This renewed vision of the Grace Marks story led to Atwood searching more deeply into the deaths of Thomas Kinnear and Nancy Montgomery along with the imprisonment of Grace Marks and the hanging of James McDermott. The novel forced Atwood to go "back to the past," which included a new series of problems: "The past is made of paper" (p. 172). Newspapers and journals and letters—this past Atwood found also uncovered the many different versions of that past and the even more puzzling conflicting stories and gaps in it. "If you're after the truth, the whole and detailed truth, and nothing but the truth, you're going to have a thin time of it if you trust to paper; but with the past, it's almost all you've got," she claims, exposing our weak grip on truth and facts (pp. 172–173).

As she continues to reveal her writing of *Alias Grace,* Atwood makes a number of observations that are truly relevant for our students today. One is her noting the *lack* of consistency in the details of the trial itself. That was traced to the journalism of 1843: "I discovered as I read that the newspapers of the time had their own polit-ical agendas" (p. 173). Yes—in 1843, journalism was both biased and political. In today's popular mythology, many on the Right have waged a successful campaign to paint the "media" as liberal, thus unfairly biased (unlike the good ol' days, the implication). What our students should recognize is that all media—in the past, today—are inherently biased; as Atwood has offered in most of her works, objectivity is not attainable. Connected with this essay, students should be asked to look closely at contemporary journalism and the messages sent concerning truth and fairness by TV, radio, and print media. (See Thomas, 2006; Chapter Two of the Vonnegut volume in this series concerning New Journalism.)

As she ends her essay, Atwood explains that she makes Marks a storyteller herself, "with strong motives to narrate, but also strong motives to withhold" (p. 174). This leads to her explaining her com-plex view of truth—"[T]ruth is sometimes unknowable, at least by us" (p. 175). And despite her postmodern views, Atwood comes to the conclusion that storytelling ultimately is about the universals, what she calls "Ancient Mariner stories" dealing with the Seven Deadly Sins and a whole host of motifs we find again and again in our histories and our mythologies and our fictions (p. 175).

This brings us to the novel itself, which Stein (1999) notes "appears very different from Atwood's previous novels" because "Grace Marks is an impoverished nineteenth-century woman who spends many years in prison" (p. 103). The humor and themes prove, however, this is the Atwood we can expect, although part of that is, with Atwood, readers should expect the unexpected. Atwood returns to gothic elements and themes about storytelling, truth, and impris-onment while weaving a fictional account of Grace Marks that is just slightly more complex than the historical Grace Marks.

Some of the elements of the novel we can address in our classes that have not been addressed in the discussion of Atwood's essay on historical fiction include the multi-genre approach she implements in the novel. Atwood writes a ballad along with letters to infuse the novel with historical weight. Her attention to detail and conventions bound by time are valuable lessons to share with students, who themselves should be asked to write in styles that reflect different times and pur-poses. Further, Atwood includes courtroom drama, romance/courtship subplots, and class conflicts in her novel as part of the traditions of Gothic works.

Alias Grace also does not fail to raise issues about class and gen-der, both literally in the 1800s setting of the novel and indirectly in our lives today. Grace is imprisoned by her life circumstances long before she finds herself in prison, for example. Having come from

Ireland, Grace is denied education and expected to subjugate herself to both men and her employers. Part of the novel, then, narrates the evolution of Grace as an empowered woman, ironically as she finds herself literally in prison. Yet, that empowerment, seemingly supported by Mary Whitney in the novel, is also questionable because we have trouble knowing the truth about Grace's role in the murders and her own veracity as a storyteller.

Finally, although it is impossible to exhaust all we can do with this novel in our classes, Atwood again makes her central character an artist. Grace is a storyteller and a quilt maker: "The chapter titles, named after quilt patterns, suggest mystery and menace" (Stein, 1999, p. 107). The quilting gives the novel structure, and it infuses Atwood's thematic concerns for art and weaving together of details to reach the truth (or some version of that truth). "Grace's story is the novel's core," Stein explains, "but it is always suspect" (p. 107).

CONNECTION

Set itself in a turbulent historical context, the 1960s and 1970s United States when race and gender were boiling at the surface of daily life, Alice Walker's "Everyday Use" is a perfect connection with Atwood's *Alias Grace* as both works implement quilting motifs to address issues of art, culture, and history in their narratives. Walker's story is well crafted and rich with her own arguments about the nature of art and the racial/gender politics of the story's setting. Students have also responded well to the story, although they generally need sufficient background information on the nuances of the historical setting of the story in order to recognize Walker's political themes. The family themes also add a powerful dynamic to the story that is appreciated by students.

After *Alias Grace*, Atwood returns to the villainess main character, Iris Griffen in *The Blind Assassin*, a work that challenges the reader again as Iris is drawn to be both repelling and attractive.

Of Words and Death—*The Blind Assassin* as Dark Fiction

The Blind Assassin (2000) offers readers another rendition of Atwood's villainess novels—this work "revers[ing] our expectations about plot" (Stein, 1999, p. 137). The work includes multiple stories, including a novel-within-a-novel as in *Lady Oracle* and Atwood's infusing her narrative with many different genres, such as newspaper clippings. As a relatively new work, this novel has received less critical attention than other novels, but it suits our classes well.

In this section, I will look briefly at the narrative structure of the novel, the thematic concerns of Atwood, and a series of intertextual readings available with the work (Cooke, 2004). Before we consider these, however, I should note that the novel focuses on Iris Griffen, and it challenges the reader on issues of villainy and perceptions of reality, issues found in the other novels discussed above.

Cooke (2004) identifies three narratives driving *The Blind Assassin,* narratives that address the dominant concerns in the novel for "the themes of blind assassins and sacrificed maidens" (p. 147). Three stories told, of course, raise the readers' awareness of perceptions of reality, of the interwoven nature of truth and story. The first narrative is Iris's confessional story, a story of her life from 1916 until 1999 and a story of the primary villainess; here, Atwood challenges the reader by creating an engaging primary character who is also replete with repellent qualities. The second narrative is the novel-within-the-novel, also titled *The Blind Assassin.* That novel is a consideration of genre by Atwood, and it forces the readers' views of reality as readers discover that the novel's author is actually Iris and not Laura Chase. The third narrative also involves genre as it is the science-fiction fantasy dealing directly with blind assassins and sacrificed maidens. The multi-layered narrative of this novel continues to emphasize key thematic concerns found in Atwood, directly manipulating how readers view plot and storytelling by the storytelling itself.

The themes addressed by Atwood through these narratives include "mass murder," "death as a kind of escape," and "the power of the word itself" (Cooke, 2004, p. 150). These themes are reinforced, of course, by the narrative itself, but Atwood also enriches those themes through several other techniques, including:

- The historical elements of the novel—Atwood confronts social issues such as class tension and working class labor in the background of Iris's life. She also alludes to classic motifs of history and mythology, a hallmark of Atwood's fiction (Cooke, 2004).
- Iris's name supports an eye motif or a sight motif that runs through the narratives as they explore how any character (or any person) "sees" reality.
- Images of a disembodied hand establish the hand as a motif, lending the novel thematic structure.
- Escape is expressed through both suicide and fantasy, mixing the dark elements and the romantic elements found in the novel.
- Similar to the quilting motif of *Alias Grace,* a button motif runs throughout *The Blind Assassin,* suggesting "an image of something that stands at the point at which different pieces of material come together or move apart" (Cooke, 2004, p. 151).

CONNECTION

Atwood never shies away from confronting traditional assumptions and traditional patterns in our society and in our literary conventions. In *The Blind Assassin,* her theme of suicide/death as escape can be found in many works addressing the oppression of women. Kate Chopin's work often explores marriage as prison for women. *The Awakening* ends with the suicide of the main character, seemingly that is her act of empowerment. How we respond as readers and people to such conflicting thematic expressions is often a point of contention. For Atwood, these patterns and conventions continue to fascinate her as an artist and a feminist, while she is notably non-conforming in both capacities. Chopin and Atwood are interesting to pair as two feminist writers separated by a century.

Finally, in this discussion of *The Blind Assassin,* I want to highlight the intertextual readings recommended by Cooke (2004), since her discussion supports an idea I have recommended through my volumes in this series (See the "Entry Points" and "Connections"). Here, briefly, I will highlight the many texts Cooke feels are companions to Atwood's *The Blind Assassin* because "the contemporary [author decides] to signal a comparison with and then deviate from the inherited script" (p. 151):

- Ovid's *Metamorphoses*
- Alfred Lord Tennyson's *Idylls of the King*
- William Wordsworth
- William Shakespeare's *King Lear*
- Samuel Taylor Coleridge's "Kubla Khan"
- Virgil's *Aeneid*
- Sophocles' *Electra and Antigone*
- Three Canadian works: Carol Shields's *The Stone Diaries*, Margaret Laurence's *The Stone Angel,* and Alice Munro's "Something I've Been Meaning to Tell You."

Stories that Don't Hold Water—
The Penelopiad as Myth Recast

In her "Introduction" to *The Penelopiad,* Atwood writes about Penelope, Odysseus' "quintessential faithful wife," "But Homer's *Odyssey* is not the only version of the story" (pp. xiii, xiv). As we have seen in many of her works, Atwood is fascinated by mythical patterns and by the pursuit of questions through fictional narratives. In *The Penelopiad,* then, she "[chooses] to give the telling of the story to Penelope and to the twelve hanged maids," and she explores "two questions that must pose themselves after any close reading of *The Odyssey:* what led to the hanging of the maids, and what was Penelope really up to?" (p. xv). Here, we will discuss bringing this novel and others into our classrooms as ways to read and re-read classic myth and legends.

ENTRY POINT

Southern culture has a long and interesting oral tradition. Whether you have experienced the South firsthand or simply found yourself in William Faulkner's fictional South, you have been exposed to the myths, fables, and legends that weave their way throughout this region of the U.S. REM, a Southern alternative-rock band, released *Fables of the Reconstruction* in 1985, their third full-length album. This work used the title to manipulate several aspects of the South—the "fables," the Reconstruction after the Civil War, and the turning back on itself of the title (alternatively read "Fables of the Reconstruction" and "Reconstruction of the Fables"). As an artistic expression, this album parallels Atwood's concern for fables and legends along with her tendency to play with words. One of the singles from that album, "Maps and Legends," is a perfect entry point to a novel unit addressing recasting classic fables, legends, and myths. In "Myths and Legends," the lyrics refer literally to a local artist, Rev. Howard Finster, but lines such as, "Maybe these maps and legends/ have been misunderstood," echo lyricist Michael Stipe's exploration of interpretations of art and legend that parallel Atwood's novel.

Atwood's *The Penelopiad* already has interesting company in many reading lists of high school and college English courses. I see this recent work by Atwood as anchoring a set of three novels to be studied in a class as a way to examine closely the value of myth, legends, and fables in any generation. Along with John Gardner's *Grendel* and John Updike's *The Centaur,* students can read these three novels in order to enrich their knowledge of classic literature while also expanding their experiences by looking critically at the patterns and motifs of narrative.

In *The Penelopiad,* Atwood recasts *The Odyssey* by shifting the narration of this classic story to Penelope and her twelve hanged maids. John Gardner shifts narrative perspective in *Grendel* by having the infamous monster of *Beowulf* tell this traditional work of English literature. Exploring the patterns of classical mythology, Updike's *The Centaur* weaves the myths of Chiron and Prometheus into his novel about a teacher and his son caught together for three days in a snowstorm.

ENTRY POINT

If we want to help students establish or refine their ability to draw meaning from the use of mythic patterns and allusion in modern narratives, John Updike's engaging and popular short story, "A&P," is an excellent way to discuss the use of myth in fiction. In this short story about a young man's confrontation with the adult world, Updike integrates allusions to the three Muses as teenage young women who enter the grocery store and set the main character's epiphany in motion.

As a novel unit of three works directly dependent on legend and myth to structure the authors' purposes, we could have students focus on the following either as a whole-class assignment or as group work to be completed outside of class:

- Research and explore the foundational legends and myths of these three novels: *Beowulf, The Odyssey,* and the myths of Chiron and Prometheus.
- Identify the direct use of these legends and myths in the novels. How do the legends and myths support larger purposes by the writers?
- Identify how each writer manipulates and confronts these legends and myths, recasting classic patterns and assumptions in their own work.
- Select other legends or myths to use as a source for writing their own original narratives.
- How do these three works differ in their approaches to themes related to gender since Atwood is the lone female writer in this grouping of works?

This unit is ripe for many reading and writing objectives in our classes. The richness of the works themselves along with the many connections these modern writers fuse with classic works makes this an exciting and foundational unit for our classrooms as we continue to seek ways in which to help our students see the value of literature for them now and always.

Chapter Five has looked closely at a series of works by Atwood that challenge the nature of truth, particularly the nature of truth as found in *text.* Atwood has questioned how we know what we know, and she has explored that concern through the act of storytelling—as well as the multiple versions of those stories that exist simultaneously. Stein (1999) explains, "Storytelling raises the question of the author's control over her text," adding, "once the story is told, the teller loses control, giving up her power to the reader or listener" (p. 87).

As teachers of English, we should see here that the later novels of Atwood fit well into our classes *if* we are seeking and embracing both reading and writing as creative acts (Rosenblatt, 1995). "A lot of lies. They said in the newspapers that I was illiterate, but I could read some even then," Grace Marks, in *Alias Grace,* reveals, weaving together the nature of truth as told through words. What could be more important for our students to confront in our classes?

Entry Points and Connections

"Tricks with Mirrors," Margaret Atwood

King Lear, William Shakespeare

Macbeth, William Shakespeare

A Tribe Apart, Patricia Hersch

The Robber Bridegroom, Eudora Welty

The Brothers Grimm, Terry Gilliam, dir.

You Can't Be Neutral on a Moving Train, Howard Zinn

Slaughterhouse-Five, Kurt Vonnegut

The Scarlet Letter, Nathaniel Hawthorne

The Crucible, Arthur Miller

"Everyday Use," Alice Walker

The Awakening, Kate Chopin

"Maps and Legends," REM, *Fables of the Reconstruction*

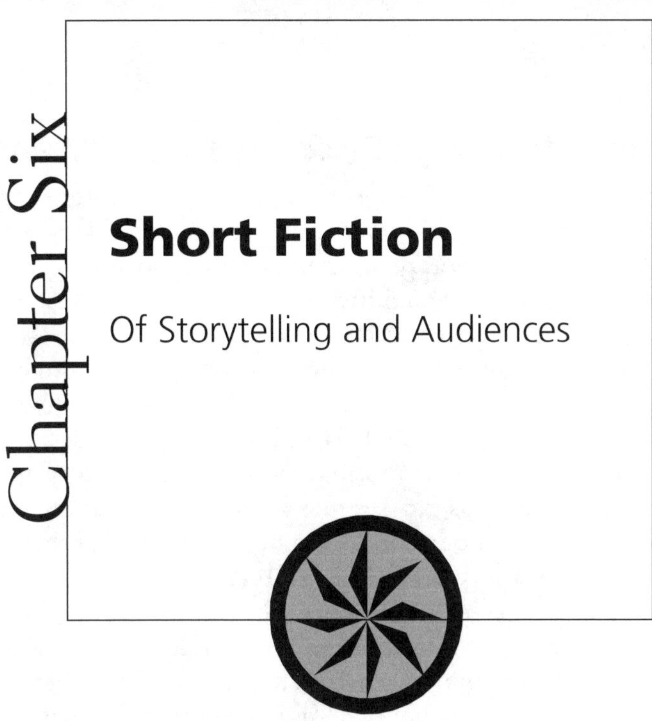

Chapter Six

Short Fiction

Of Storytelling and Audiences

"Why do people tell stories, 'real' stories or 'made up' stories, and why do people listen to them?" asks Atwood (1982) in "An End to Audience?" from *Second Words* (p. 337). In this extended consideration of being a writer and writing, of the commercialism of writing, and of the potential loss of writing *if* the audience truly doesn't care, Atwood is forcing her audience to consider whether or not the act of storytelling is something valuable—whether or not storytelling is something inherent in being human, even. Of all the genres, students might be most comfortable with and accustomed to the reading and writing of short stories. I have found that we seem to believe that making up stories is not only a fair thing to ask of students but also easily done.

Yet, I argue that creating a story *and* crafting that story is a daunting task—one that is probably beyond many of our students. That said, studying the short story form, since it is brief and fulfilling as a form (similar in many respects to a poem), is an important part of the English curriculum. Here, we will explore Atwood's discussions of the short story along with several of her wonderful stories. First, we will use Atwood's writing about short stories as grounding for exploring the form. Next, we will look closely at "The War in the Bathroom," "Rape Fantasies," "The Resplendent Quetzal," and "Dancing Girls" as studies in specific short stories and related themes. Briefly, before moving to her poetry, I will discuss having students experiment with writing short stories themselves.

How to Judge Short Stories—"Reading Blind"

Stein (1999) notes that Atwood's short stories "combine realism and whimsy, fairy tale, myth, and fantasy as they represent the lives of contemporary women and men struggling to cope with an often puzzling and difficult world" (p. 125). These qualities are common throughout much of Atwood's works; for our students, then, we need to examine closely how the short story form itself impacts both her themes and her craft. The ideal way to explore short stories is through Atwood's "Reading Blind," included in her *Writing with Intent* (2005). This musing about the short story form gives her reader insight as it raises many questions about the form and composing.

For our classes, the first two-thirds of this essay is ideal; we can certainly leave out the reading of the final third, which directly addresses the stories she helps select for *The Best American Short Stories 1989* (although it would make sense to include one of these stories in our unit on the short story). Immediately, Atwood begins by expressing her own discomfort with evaluating and judging the relative quality of any short story. For her, as an artist, she clearly bristles at judging any art form by prescriptions: "The word *should* is a dangerous one to use when speaking of writing. It's a kind of challenge to the deviousness and inventiveness and audacity and perversity of the creative spirit" (p. 68).

When I first read this brilliant and apt comment by Atwood, I thought of a story about Flannery O'Connor; it is one of those stories that may *not* be historically accurate, but it is so good, it is worth risking. It appears that many of O'Connor's best-known and most well-regarded works are driven by her desire to refute a common piece of advice for novice fiction writers: Avoid clichés; thus, stories such as "A Good Man Is Hard to Find." Atwood continues early in her essay, "We don't judge good stories by the application to them of some set of external measurements, as we judge giant pumpkins at the fall fair" (p. 68). I cannot stress enough here that Atwood is raising some crucial issues with her comments. With art, our evaluations must work from the story outward—not by approaching each story with a prescription, then merely checking off how many characteristics each story fulfills.

First, most English courses *hand* to students year after year a series of implicitly teacher-endorsed works, and thus students never have an opportunity to develop a sense of judgment themselves or explicitly explore just how we decide whether a piece of writing is "good" or not. *"Young Goodman Brown" is a great short story because it is written by Nathaniel Hawthorne and because it is assigned in English class—both reasons contribute negatively to the development of our students as readers and writers.* Since short stories are brief and probably less daunting than poems, we could use the study of short stories to allow students opportunities to judge the quality of literature. One way to explore judging stories is the following:

- Divide the class into several groups of about 3 to 5 students each.
- Prepare for each group a set of stories *with no designation of the author on the stories.* The stories you select should be fairly brief and works students have never seen before. Some stories you might want to consider include:

  - "The Use of Force," William Carlos Williams
  - "The Story of an Hour," Kate Chopin
  - "Harrison Bergeron," Kurt Vonnegut
  - "Extinctions," Barbara Kingsolver
  - "The Lesson," Toni Cade Bambara
  - "A Good Man Is Hard to Find," Flannery O'Connor
  - "Araby," James Joyce
  - "One Holy Night," Sandra Cisneros
  - "Rules of the Game," Amy Tan

This list could go on forever, but you simply need to collect three or four stories per group (groups could share the same stories or the stories could be unique to each group).

- Assign each group to *rank* these stories from best to worst (or some sort of ranking). Each group must establish how they have given those rankings; press the groups to be very specific in their judgments.
- Twists on this assignment can include planting one terrible story in each group. *Finding* bad fiction will be a challenge, but what you will be seeking is probably genre fiction that is cliché ridden (in ways distinct from O'Connor) ineffective, and formulaic.

This activity is based on Atwood's metaphor of "reading blind"; when she chose stories for the collection, the authors' names were omitted: "I had been freed from the weight of authorial reputation" (p. 69). Further, this process depends on valuing the discussions within the groups and the criteria the groups establish from those discussions. The groups should be pursuing Atwood's questions: "What would be my criteria, if any? How would I be able to tell the best from the merely better? How would I *know?*" (p. 69).

While this process addresses our students' development as readers, it is also contributing to the evolving rubrics they are creating in their minds *as writers.* In Atwood's discussion, she is offering her view of the short story as both expert reader and writer. Since Atwood offers her own criteria for judging stories—although she raises more questions than offering strict "rules"—we might have students do the above activity before they read this essay; then they could compare their criteria to Atwood's.

The first quality Atwood values—"What makes a good story a unified whole, something complete and satisfying in itself?" (p. 70)—is the "voice of the story." She explains that "[o]ur first stories come to us through the air. We hear voices" (p. 71). The oral nature of storytelling is traced to the childhood of nearly all of us who have been read stories, who have stories of our families told to us over and over. Atwood notes the value of religious stories, fairy tales, and children's books (see Chapter Eight), but she also acknowledges that our childlike wonder that embraces such storytelling is usually erased as we grow older; thus, we often come to undervalue both stories and writers.

Connected to the voice of the story, according to Atwood, is that "language, including the language of our earliest-learned stories, is a verbal matrix, not a verbal patrix," since children most often hear stories from the mouths of the women in their lives ("nursery tales or old wives' tales," we call them) (p. 72). From these heard stories, we begin to shape our sense of what stories should do, how stories can be fulfilling to the reader in a permanent form, thus written. Atwood believes writers are those people "who never kicked the habit. We remained tale-bearers. We learned to keep our eyes open, but not to keep our mouths shut" (p. 72).

Before moving on to her second broad principle, we should consider the double use of the word "voice" in our discussions of stories with our students. Here, Atwood has emphasized literally how stories sound aloud. And we should add this element to the drafting process of our students—reading a work aloud for oneself, reading a draft aloud for an audience. But we also need to explore with our students how we identify in a work as readers and how we create in a work a writers' *voice*. When we address writers' voice as a craft, we are not discussing how the writing sounds aloud, but the rhythms and qualities of the words and sentences *on the page*. This is a challenging concept; here are some guiding elements that we can consider, however, to help students develop a sense of voice:

- Voice in writing is related to the level of formality in a written piece. Generally, we can ask students to identify where on a spectrum from informal to formal a work fits. Of course, identifying the formality of a written piece comes with experience. For example, we can have students place "cranium," "head," and "noggin" in their order of formality as a way to help them begin to consider this evaluation of writing.

- Voice—as with formality—is directly related to the diction (word choice) of a piece. Novice writers often fail to maintain control of the level of diction in their writing, often switching among words that contrast each other in the voice they create and the formality they suggest; this switching is a problem for student writers because there is no *purpose* in the choices. Many students will seek a thesaurus and simply choose words from the list—making no consideration of voice, tone, or appropriateness of the choices.
- Also related to voice is syntax and sentence formation. The order of words within a sentence along with the sentence length and sentence length variety of a piece creates voice. Generally, this can be demonstrated for students by showing them simple examples of how we react to the same words in different order: Compare "Through the door he did walk" with "He did walk through the door."

We must help students as readers and writers see that control of voice and purposefulness of voice are vital to judging a story as fulfilling or not, thus "good" or a failure.

"In fiction, however, excellence resides in divergence, or how else could we be surprised? Hence the trickiness of the formulations," Atwood explains as she moves to her second parameter for judging stories, "[t]he uncertainty principle . . . : *You can say why a story is bad, but it's much harder to say why it's good*" (p. 73). Similar to some of Kurt Vonnegut's discussions of his own craft as a writer of fiction (Thomas, 2006), Atwood argues, "It's in this last respect that the story (as distinct from the novel) comes closest to resembling two of its oral predecessors, the riddle and the joke" (p. 74). Vonnegut and Atwood share a belief that fiction and the success of fiction depend heavily on "the same impeccable sense of timing" found in the joke (p. 74). Stories, in a wide variety of ways, establish some expectations in readers and then, again in a variety of ways, fulfills those expectations by either going where the reader expects in some interesting way or by surprising the reader in some interesting way.

Continuing to express her own inadequacy as a judge of short stories, Atwood culminates her discussion of "the uncertainty principle" by arguing for the value of "urgency" in the telling of a story: "It must be told with as much intentness as if the teller's life depended on it" (p. 75). I would argue that Atwood is using "urgency" to suggest impassioned *purposefulness* in both meaning and craft. Before she discusses the stories she chose for this collection, a section we could skip with our students, she offers an idea that parallels Rosenblatt (1995), who sees the act of reading as creative: "Their [the audiences'] act of listening is its reincarnation" (p. 75). This leaves us with having students consider what role the reader plays in determining the value of any story—suggesting the subjective nature of judging any art.

In many of her discussions of storytelling, Atwood mentions Samuel Taylor Coleridge's "The Rime of the Ancient Mariner." This classic work is perfect to include in our consideration of storytelling as it involves telling a story of a story telling, paralleling many of Atwood's works that include stories within stories (*Lady Oracle, The Robber Bride*). Coleridge's work raises the issue of storytellers feeling *compelled* to tell their stories; it also can lead to discussion of how we value the stories themselves in relationship to the themes those stories suggest. The storyteller or writer will often value the story itself while in academic settings we tend to gravitate toward discussing the themes as if they are more valuable than the storytelling.

The Split Self—"The War in the Bathroom"

Stein (1999) explains that "The War in the Bathroom," the opening story of *Dancing Girls* (1977), "sets the book's tone of claustrophobia and despair and introduces the first of its double protagonists" (p. 127). This story represents Atwood's interest in multiple realities, as we see in her other works, and multiple versions of "the story," but here she looks at multiple views of the world from inside a single character whose psyche appears fractured: "This protagonist is explicitly split into two, a speaking voice and an acting person" (Stein, p. 127).

Edgar Allan Poe's "William Wilson" shares the split narrator with Atwood's "The War in the Bathroom." As paired works, these stories consider the possibility of the fractured self, the fragmented psyche. Many works of literature explore this element of being human, often by directly or indirectly incorporating the Freudian concept of the id, ego, and superego. The psychology of these terms is distinct from the use of the concepts in literature; students often benefit from making those distinctions while using the Freudian framework to structure how they interpret literature.

Beyond the element of the split psyche of the narrator, this story offers several other avenues for discussion:

- The story is divided into sections titled by days of the week—Monday through Sunday. Students can examine how this framing device contributes to the work. They could also write their own fictional pieces implementing some similar framing device.

- Many of the stories in *Dancing Girls* include issues of foreign characters. Here, the story mentions "the German woman" early, carrying a negative tone (p. 1). How does this story explore "foreign" in both literal and figurative ways?

- The framing element of the days of the week is reinforced in the story with a "woman with two voices" motif running throughout. The use of motif along with the power of motif as an element is a valuable discussion for students who are developing their approaches to literature. Identifying repetition is crucial for understanding stories; here, the "woman with two voices" reinforces ironically that our narrator has a split psyche as we discover the woman with two voices actually *is* two women.

- The bathroom as a place of refuge and a place of privacy has resonance in the story since the narrator perceives she is fighting for that bathroom, thus a refuge and a place of privacy—possibly from the strangers and foreigners she feels surround her. Atwood returns to the bathroom as a symbolic place in her "Dancing Girls" story near the end of the collection.

Ultimately, if we return to the framing element of the days of the week, we see that the source of the narrator's fractured self may be the routine of her life, the monotony of the real world. One of the recurring concerns of Atwood's writing is her ability to explore the mundane through classic structures, her mixing of the real world with mythic patterns. In a short story, that craft is often subtle, but even more powerful.

The Language of Victims—"Rape Fantasies"

It is no cliché to state that artists are often ahead of their times—in terms of both social awareness and social commentary. Atwood personifies that truism. As well, appropriately for this book and this series, Atwood is often confrontational in both her perceptiveness and her criticisms of us as humans. In *The Handmaid's Tale,* she has a flashback scene when Offred/June and her friend Moira discuss date rape, making disturbing jokes about the term sounding like a dessert. Atwood also creates tension and discomfort for her reader in that same novel with the sex act during the Ceremony (along with Offred/June's language while describing the act) and the brutal murder of the accused rapist by the handmaids. In her first collection of stories,

Dancing Girls, "Rape Fantasies" offers the reader similar discomfort within a highly crafted work.

"Rape Fantasies" addresses two provocative and unnerving concepts through the narration of a secretary out on a date—whether or not women actually fantasize about being raped and the threat of date rape (also called "acquaintance rape"). While the concept of rape fantasies was nothing new in the 1960s and 1970s, discussions about date rape were becoming popular through women's magazines and other forms of popular media by the mid-1970s. Atwood's brilliant story unfolds a horrific tale through a masterful use of narration that captures a character telling a story while the reader infers the larger story of that character's possible predicament.

Stein (1999) believes the story raises a question about the power of the main character's story that she is telling. Literally, the reader discovers just past the middle of the story that the narrator is talking to her date: "But I guess it's different for a guy" (p. 99). Until this point, it appears that the narrator is simply musing about her conversations with her friends concerning the silly fantasies that they have shared with each other about being raped—or actually about rape fantasies that are almost anything except rape. The scenarios the narrator is sharing are both humorous and oddly touching, seemingly a parody by Atwood of the Romance convention of the raped damsel who falls in love with her captor. When the reader recognizes this nonstop monologue about *rape* is being told to some unnamed and briefly mentioned date, the tone of the story changes dramatically. The rape fantasies contrast sharply with the danger the narrator *might* be facing—or at least appears to be anticipating.

Seemingly, the humor and the compassion in the fantasies the narrator is sharing may be designed by that narrator as a shield against the danger her date poses (Stein, 1999). Since the entire story, however, is the non-stop monologue by the narrator, the reader is left with many options. One scenario could be that the narrator is *imagining* the threat due to her having discussed similar topics with her friends or having read about date rape in a magazine. A second scenario could be that the power of her stories does create a bond between her and the date, preventing the man from raping her. Third, the threat and rape could be real and impending no matter what she does. The tension of the story comes from the open-ended resolution to the situation. We are left without any way to know the reality. Just one sentence from the end of the story, in fact, the narrator poses a question—and then offers her confusion about date rape: "I mean, I know it happens but I just don't understand it, that's the part I really don't understand" (p. 103).

For our classes, this story offers a number of lessons revolving around both the craft of the story and the topics the story raises. First, the story itself is a tour de force of narration and the adage "Show; don't tell." Atwood creates tension by having the narrator placed in a situation where everything the reader needs is revealed through her monologue; the monologue itself is showing since it is a real act by a character. If we have had our students experiment with evaluating short stories, as outlined above, this story would be ideal for discussing how a story achieves success through qualities that are often found in strong fiction: The story is fulfilling; the story creates tension in the reader; the story provides the readers with all the information they need and the story is both topical and universal.

The topical nature of the story also creates opportunities for valuable lessons that are relevant to high school and college students. Date rape and the issues of violence between women and men who know each other are important topics for young people to face. This story can provide opportunities for our students to research date rape as well as discuss the pressures and power balances that occur between men and women in intimate relationships.

Another topic that may seem less dramatic to our students is the debate the story raises over the power of language and the power of story. The narrator appears to be using the act of storytelling to create a bond between her and her date, a bond that she hopes will humanize her for him and thus protect her from a rape. As well, the stories she tells are filled with humor and compassion, suggesting that the content of stories itself can impact the audience of those stories. Atwood often asks her readers to consider the power of both language and stories; the open-ended nature of this disturbing story is ripe for that debate.

Loveless Marriage and Loss—
"The Resplendent Quetzal"

"Their life together is built of avoidance, indirection, evasion, and outright dishonesty," explains Stein (1999, p. 129) about the main characters in Atwood's "The Resplendent Quetzal." Reminding the reader of Kate Chopin's portrayal of marriage as a prison, Atwood's story explores the life of Sarah and Edward, a couple left hollow by the loss of a child at birth. The story opens ominously: "Sarah was sitting near the edge of the sacrificial well" (p. 152). Words such as "sacrificial" and "edge" establish the tension and the death of the love and the marriage between Sarah and Edward.

CONNECTION

Ernest Hemingway's "Hills like White Elephants" shares with Atwood's "Rape Fantasies" brilliant narrative technique; Hemingway's camera point of view (a narration that is nearly without evaluation, nearly without emotion as a video camera catching an extended scene) is masterful, and like Atwood's monologue in "Rape Fantasies," the point of view contributes to the gradual realization by the reader of Hemingway's topic and the tension in the story. However, "Hills like White Elephants" shares its theme with "The Resplendent Quetzal," as both stories look at the loss of love and affection as that loss grows from the pregnancy of the woman in the relationship; in Hemingway's story the couple is ruined by their disagreement over an abortion, while in Atwood's story, the loss of the baby in childbirth kills that couple's reason for being together.

Immediately after the ominous first sentence, the reader finds that Sarah "had imagined something smaller, more like a wishing well" (p. 152). These opening sentences juxtapose "sacrifice," "edge," and "wishing," establishing the tension of the story between the reality of our lives and all that we wish for. As with other stories in *Dancing Girls,* Atwood places this story of lost love and hollow marriage in the context of foreigners and strangers; they are surrounded by other tourists, and the narration notes nationalities often, especially in the beginning. This story explores a sense of alienation both as a fact of human existence and as an element of marriage.

Similar to the simmering violence in *The Handmaid's Tale* and "Rape Fantasies," the reader discovers Sarah's loss of interest in Edward's obsessions—especially since he seems to have replaced her with bird watching—and then is jolted by Edward's fantasy: "Edward had a sudden image of himself, crashing out of the undergrowth like King Kong, picking Sarah up and hurling her over the edge, down into the sacrificial well" (pp. 156–157). This perverse fantasy fulfills the ominous tone of the first sentence and creates tension and irony for the reader who is aware of this fantasy while the couple walks through the story maintaining their facades for each other.

Soon after Edward's fantasy, the reader learns of the baby dying at birth; then Sarah contemplates completing the trip "if Edward had conveniently died" (p. 159). While both characters have violent fantasies, Atwood has presented the reader with Edward dramatically *taking* his wife's life and Sarah passively contemplating Edward's "convenient" and unspecified death. Here, we can discuss the association of violence with gender. After the narration reveals Sarah has considered cheating on her husband, but never following through, the violent element in the story returns with ornamental figures from the manger scene and the tour guide's discussion of sacrificing virgins as a part of a religious act. Throughout this scene, two women on the tour repeatedly include "'beats me'" in their conversation, reinforcing the violence motif in the diction of the story (p. 162).

The story returns to the death of the couple's child. The narration seems to suggest that it is not simply the death of the child that also kills their love and marriage. Sarah is alone when she learns of the child's death, and Edward is "the one who had cried, not Sarah. She had never cried" (p. 165). This section of the story also explores the couple's love and marriage being tied directly to Sarah's pregnancy and to the dull hope that a new child might rekindle their love and marriage, like "[a] jewel, a precious feather" (p. 165). This image is fulfilled by the climax of the story.

Sarah has stolen the baby Jesus figure from the ornamental manger scene earlier. The fable of the Virgin Birth, the perfection of Jesus, both are weaved in the narration that discusses Sarah "tak[ing] meticulous care of herself" during her pregnancy and even her habitual smoothing of her skirt to keep it looking perfect (p. 166). In this section detailing her stealing the baby Jesus figure, the reader also learns that Sarah has been taking her birth control pills secretly, spoiling Edward's fantasy that a new child would save their marriage. When Edward walks up on Sarah at "the well's edge" again, she is "paralyzed" and "immobile" (p. 167). Then, she "drew back her right arm and threw something into the well" (p. 167).

The story ends after this scene of Sarah throwing away the baby Jesus figure with Edward struggling against Sarah crying: "The ordinary Sarah . . . was something he could cope with. . . . But he was unprepared for this. She had always been the one in control" (p. 168). The ending is eerie as Sarah regains her normal face, "smooth[s] her skirt once more," and states that she wants an orange (p. 168). The facades return for the couple, but the reader is left with knowing what lies beneath it all. "The implication is that their marriage will continue, sterile and suffocating," explains Stein (1999, p. 129).

Fearing that which Is Foreign— "Dancing Girls"

"[T]he new man" of the collection's title story, "Dancing Girls," is portrayed as foreign and tattooed to Ann by her landlady, the story echoing the motifs of violence and rape along with the use of the bathroom found in other stories. Here, the story raises a question about human nature: Do we gravitate toward the familiar and fear the foreign?

The story focuses on Ann and her life in her apartment that shares a bathroom with another apartment. The narration is limited omniscient; the reader has the details about Ann's life and the mysterious new man, who will share Ann's bathroom (a place of refuge and privacy as we have seen in "The War in the Bathroom"), gradually revealed. As well, rape, murder, and the references to foreigners create a threatening tone surrounding the beginning pages of the story while the reader is learning about Ann's friendship with the former tenant, Lelah. When the landlady tells Ann the new man is both "'from one of them Arabian countries'" and "'He's got these tattoo marks on his face. . . . But he's real nice'" (p. 211). This exchange includes the landlady acknowledging she feels close to Ann because Ann isn't foreign (although Ann *is* foreign, but remains silent just as she fails to act at the end of the story).

The story begins to build a color motif that establishes the color green with Ann's quest to practice Urban Design, including her wish to "rearrange Toronto" (p. 215). Ann is shown to be struggling with the apparent inequity of actually implementing the theory of Urban Design into the lives of real people as that parallels with her meeting the new man, who appears lonely to her and who has scarring on his face instead of tattoos. The story returns again and again to Ann's "green spaces" throughout the rest of the story, preparing the reader for the final paragraph that follows the climax of the main story concerning the new man. Scenes of Ann wrestling with the concept of "exclusive" and with Jetske accusing her of being a socialist create in the story a tension between the theoretical and the real. While Ann believes her actions of implementing Urban Design theory would be unfair to individual people, will that change what she chooses to do?

The story ends with a direct conflict between the reality of the new man's party and the landlady's latent fear of foreigners. The motifs of passivity and paralysis, also found in "The Resplendent Quetzal," are emphasized in the late scenes of the story as Ann sits in her apartment and simply listens to the party being held by the new man. The next day, her shared bathroom is filthy from the party, but Ann receives the story of the party from the landlady, raising questions about the objectivity of her version. Nonetheless, the landlady accuses the new man of having *dancing girls,* seemingly a euphemism for prostitutes, in his room, resulting in the landlady calling the police (who never come) and literally chasing the new man and his guests away.

Ann realizes the new man is actually harmless; he has been the victim of the landlady's prejudice, her self-fulfilling prophecy. As the story ends, the narration focuses on Ann not "risk[ing] opening her door" that night during the party; "if [Ann had] had the courage to look," could she or would she have intervened on the new man's behalf, the wronged man's behalf (p. 224)? The story ends with fantasy, a revised version of Ann's green space. The final green space is no longer exclusive; there is no fence in contrast to earlier in the story. The green space has animals, people holding hands happily, people in natural garb, music, and "dancing girls . . . sedately dancing" (p. 225).

While the story is compelling and well crafted, I would have students read this work in order to decipher the mythic nature of the final green space. Is this final scene a hopeful scene? What should readers take from the final image of the dancing girls dancing "sedately," paralleling the paralysis motif throughout the story?

CONNECTION

As I have noted in this chapter, the short story as a form is a highly crafted genre similar to poetry in its focus on unity and its intense craft. "Dancing Girls" works as a story significantly because of the final paragraph detailing Ann's final green space fantasy. John Gardner is notable for his craft as a writer of short stories. His "Redemption" parallels "Dancing Girls" as another short story that relies on the final scene in the last paragraph of the story. In both stories, the authors bring the reader back to motifs and themes that are reframed and open-ended. The stories also share a possible optimistic ending that might be less optimistic than the reader first thinks.

As well, "Dancing Girls" raises questions about our human nature, about how we react to both ideas and people who are foreign to us. In the first years of the twenty-first century, this is a serious concern for our students as we continue to watch the rising conflict on the world stage between radical Islamic terrorism and much of the Christian world, particularly the United States. While the specifics of the story appear to be bound by time, the story proves to be universal.

From Reading Atwood to Crafting Short Stories—Students as Writers

Students are repeatedly assigned the writing of their own original short stories; this assignment begins almost in the first days of school when students are allowed to draw their stories and continues throughout their lives as students. Yet, I am troubled by two aspects of this fact of English courses. First, writing an original short story is extremely hard—even for professional writers. Second, the assignment is often lacking in real support by the teacher, in terms of fostering the craft of writing fiction, and is often accompanied by a tacit acceptance of almost anything the student produces (which does far more harm than good for our students).

I would recommend that we either reduce greatly how often we assign the writing of original fiction by our students (or even stop the practice all together) or that we give the assignment the same rigor we expect in our essay writing assignments. *Students need and deserve direct instruction, time to draft, and assessment of their short story assignments just as they receive for their essay assignments.* Many teachers feel inadequate to respond to student "creative writing," although they will not hesitate to fail a student on a critical essay. This problem can be addressed by making two changes in our assumptions, as follows:

- We must stop referring to poetry and fiction *only* as "creative writing," we must begin seeing *all* original writing by our students as creative—regardless of genre. LaBrant (Thomas, 2001) argued many decades ago for us to reframe how we view the creativity of writing, and I agree. If we begin to emphasize the creative nature of all writing our students draft by choice, we also raise the level of our students as writers—expecting the same attention to purpose and craft in all their work.

- Then, we must realize that *all* student writing is personal, thus, if we respond with criticism on any writing by students, then we are risking impacting how our students feel. Student affect is extremely important—and oddly only recognized on "throwaway" assignments such as writing stories or poems. That is truly a disconnect. Instead, we should respect student affect by valuing all of their writing; one way to show that we value any students and their work is to hold them to high standards, to give them quality feedback, and to support them as they work to improve the effectiveness of their work.

Placing a short story writing assignment within an Atwood short story unit, I believe, is a perfect opportunity to change how we view the writing of short stories as well as how our students view that same assignment. Yet, having students write original fiction is fraught with traps that can truly ruin the positive experience we can create when reading Atwood's stories and other wonderful short fiction. Here are a few strategies to help avoid some of those traps:

- Use the examination of one of Atwood's stories as the basis for asking students to create themselves a rubric for the writing of their own stories. This helps provide students with a clear basis for their writing, and it establishes parameters for your assessment of the stories. Since students—with the input of the teacher—create the rubrics, that process can often quell any complaints from students that their stories are "personal," therefore beyond grading. *We should be careful not to expect the same rubric from class to class; as Atwood's own discussion of good short stories reveals, the act of considering what makes a story good may be more important than any set of fixed guidelines.*

- Help students prepare for the drafting of the story by asking them to complete brief and targeted writing exercises (Thomas, 2005b). Writing exercises (as opposed to composing original writing) are prompted and designed to be merely exercises (not written with the intent of drafting the piece in hopes of producing a finished product for a specific audience). These exercises should address learning to show and not to tell, incorporating craft in prose writing, creating and developing characters, establishing key elements of a story in the first sentences of the story, and other elements of short fiction that we value.

- Since students writing short stories *as an assignment* is essentially an inauthentic experience (authentic work by professional writers is produced by *choice*), we can help our students by giving them strict parameters for their work, guidelines that help them avoid typical student habits that are sure to mar their work. One guideline is to ban students from killing their main character; too often, the only tension a student builds into a story is that it leads to a tragic death or suicide of the main character. Another important guideline is to require that students base their stories on things they actually know—such as building their characters around themselves and the people in their lives and creating plots around the narratives of their own lives. Without this second guideline, students tend to rehash TV and movie plots and characters that are themselves weak. A third guideline is to frame the story for the students—such as "Place two characters in a situation that confronts them with a moral dilemma."

Writing short fiction is challenging; thus, it is valuable as a writing assignment in our classes. With a rich experience of reading and evaluating short stories, such as Atwood's, under their belts, students can produce short fiction that we and they will find interesting and even surprising.

While I have looked at only a few stories from Atwood's first collection of stories, I believe the short stories of Atwood and the short story form itself are valuable in our classrooms as they both lend themselves to challenging our students as readers and writers. I will add that, as I have suggested elsewhere (Thomas, 2006), students often benefit from reading and exploring a complete collection of stories by one writer. The discussion above shows Atwood's collections lend themselves well to this assignment. Now, in Chapter Seven, we will look at the other jewels in Atwood's canon, her poetry.

ENTRY POINTS AND CONNECTIONS

"The Rime of the Ancient Mariner," Samuel Taylor Coleridge

"William Wilson," Edgar Allan Poe

"Hills like White Elephants," Ernest Hemingway

"Redemption," John Gardner

Poetry, Of Hooks and Eyes

In an article for *English Journal* concerning teaching Emily Dickinson to high school students who often groaned when the word "poetry" was uttered, I argued that we need to convince students first that poetry is not something foreign to their lives or their ears; my technique is to explore the poetry found in song lyrics as a way to move into poetry as a genre (Thomas, 1998). Georgia Heard (1999) makes a similar, but larger argument about the value of poetry in our classrooms: "We all have poetry inside of us, and I believe that poetry is for everyone, but can we recognize it when we hear it, in our students and in ourselves?" (p. xv). Heard also regrets that students seem to immediately reject the reading and writing of poetry; she poses a possible reason: "Perhaps it's the way it has been taught and presented to us that makes so many people exclude it from their lives" (p. xvi). And I agree.

In this chapter, I will look closely at teaching poetry through the poems of Atwood. I believe, as does Heard, that poetry can be the best avenue to exploring who our students are as people and as writers. Poetry as a genre forces readers and writers to look at ideas and craft in intense and compressed ways that lend themselves to the classroom. First, I will discuss the nature of poetry—how we can reconnect our students with poetry by confronting the assumptions and misconceptions they bring to our classes. Then, I will look at Atwood's own discussions of poetry and being a poet. The rest of the chapter will be devoted to the poetry of Atwood.

Reading and Writing Poetry Again for the First Time—Assumptions and Misconceptions

For nearly twenty years of teaching high school English, I spent at least one quarter of each academic year focusing on poetry. More than a decade of that career was mired in my searching for a perfect formula, for a perfect definition of poetry that I could *give* my students that would somehow magically transform them into lovers of poetry—or even poets. Since formulas and definitions were my goals, it was a doomed experiment (consider Atwood's comments about judging short stories). What I learned instead was that the students themselves had to be asked and allowed to pursue poetry *themselves.* That involved me asking, repeatedly, "What makes poetry *poetry?*" It also involved convincing students they did know that answer (although primarily intuitively) and that they have many assumptions and misconceptions about poetry we were going to have to address.

Since our high school and college students enter our English courses with many years of reading and considering poetry already behind them, we can quickly address both what they know, what they assume, and what they misunderstand about poetry. A simple opening activity is to turn to a page in a textbook that includes both prose and poetry. This should be done quickly, without allowing time for any actual reading; ask students to identify where there is poetry on the page. Virtually every time, students can identify the poem simply from *how poetry looks on the page.* Here, we uncover their intuitive sense of the central aspect of poetry that distinguishes it from other genres: *Our ultimate quest in the teaching of poetry is to raise students' awareness as both readers and writers of the inherent purposefulness of forming lines and stanzas in poetry as distinct from composing in sentences and paragraphs (prose).*

After establishing that students have the essential awareness of the poetic form, we must immediately turn to the more difficult aspects of reading and writing poetry—those negative associations students often have with the form, as noted by Heard (1999). While we want to build on their ability to *see* poetry by bringing in both songs (which triggers their poetic ear) and children's literature (which triggers their childlike wonder for language and its rhythms), we also want to uncover their academic and formal assumptions and misconceptions that are often clouding those eyes and ears that will allow them to embrace poetry more fully and willingly. The uncovering of those assumptions and misconceptions must happen as we are developing and reforming their poetic sensibilities, but we can begin by simply asking, "What makes poetry *poetry?*" They keep their initial comments and return to them throughout the studying of poetry, with an eye toward restating their answer toward the end of a poetry unit.

The assumptions and misconceptions we uncover will vary, but I can assure you that some of them will include the following:

- Students maintain a strong association between rhyme and poetry; ironically, they often exhibit the worst possible proclivities toward writing poetry that rhymes *poorly.* The key to this element of poetic sensibility is helping students develop an ear for the connection between rhyme and tone; for example, in contemporary poetry, heavy rhyme is more often found in light or humorous verse, much as it is found in children's literature. The problem with this pattern in contemporary verse is that in older poetry and in traditional forms, the heavy rhyme is couched in more serious tones. The rhyme concern is much more of a problem when helping students write poetry, however.

- Speaking of tone, students associate almost *all* literature studied in our classrooms with strictly serious topics and tones. Humor and even irony are often the last things on students' minds. They will leap on the themes related to death in Emily Dickinson, but miss entirely her sardonic tone toward conformity.

- Students also expect poetic topics to be about grand things; they miss the tendency for poetry to explore the poetic in daily and simple things.

- Students often assume the speaker in all poetry is the author. This assumption blocks their ability to see that many poems are the voice of some character (in poetry, a personae), a technique they associate with fiction.

- Students believe their poetry to be *personal,* thus they often feel teachers cannot and should not offer what they perceive as criticism; they especially balk at poetry being "graded."

- Possibly the greatest assumption that is also a misconception is that students believe poetry to be primarily abstract—the diction and the topics and themes. Since many of the poems we bring into the classroom are difficult for children and adolescents (because of the language, the topics, and the depth and breadth of the allusions and context needed to understand the poems), they begin to see the *purpose* of writing to be obscure and abstract. They believe a poem can be about "hope," but fail to see that Dickinson's "thing with feathers"; it is the bird that captures us, not the abstraction.

CONNECTION

Poets are apt not only to speak or write about poetry but also to write poems about poetry. Two poems that confront students with the nature of poetry that I have used with success in my classes are Archibald MacLeish's "Ars Poetica" (confronting the concrete nature of poetry) and Marianne Moore's "Poetry" (confronting the tension between interpreting and enjoying poetry). MacLeish bombards the reader with imagery and contradictions—such as proclaiming "[a] poem should be wordless" (1. 7) while using words in his poem. The last two lines are excellent for discussing the nature of poetry as well: "A poem should not mean/ But be." Moore also disorients her reader by opening her poem with "I, too, dislike it," referring to poetry. Eventually, the reader recognizes that the poem's speaker is tired of *interpreting* poetry, but does enjoy poetry (a circumstance we might find among our students).

- Because of how we approach poetry in our classrooms, students often see poems as simply what we use in order to do the "literary technique hunt." In other words, students read poems and list all the literary techniques they can identify—as if poets write poems just to use techniques.

With these assumptions and misconceptions in mind—and with others we will identify—we can plan our poetry lessons to help students move away from these hurdles to their embracing poetry and toward a higher poetic sensibility. A few strategies can become anchoring instructional approaches we use throughout our poetry lessons, such as the following:

- When we assign students to write poetry, we can give one restriction—no rhyme. This forces students to explore all of the other techniques writers employ when creating poems, thus helping them see beyond their limiting view of poetry as rhyming.
- Give students a strategy for approaching poetry that helps them move beyond just identifying technique. This process includes having them ask three questions—What? How? and Why? With each poem, students should consider, What is the writer doing? How is the writer doing it (technique)? and Why does it matter to the reader?
- Select poems to study that are *unlike* the poems we typically study in our classes—poetry that is humorous, poetry about highly specific and common topics, poetry that breaks conventional structures, poetry by contemporary and modern writers rarely taught in school.

And as I will discuss in the rest of this chapter, Atwood's poetry suits this goal of introducing our students to poetry again for the first time extremely well.

Atwood's Words about Poetry— The Poet, The Audience

Stein (1999) recognizes Atwood's gift for all genres of writing, but she adds that for Atwood "it was her poetry that first built her reputation" (p. 9). Her publications of poetry collections are impressive—as impressive as her canon of novels. Especially early in her career, as well, she often spoke about herself as a poet. In *Margaret Atwood: Conversations* (Ingersoll, 1990), a collection of interviews with Atwood, she offers several comments about poetry in general and about herself as a poet that gives us as teachers and our students important insights to her poems.

In an interview with Levenson, Atwood makes a distinction about confessional poets when Levenson pushes her about Sylvia Plath; in that distinction, Atwood explains that adolescents are prone to dealing in stereotypes because of their "level of writing" (Ingersoll, 1990, p. 22). In her defense of the craft in Plath, and other marginalized poets, Atwood also emphasizes the importance of the audience, of the reader. This is a key point raised often by Atwood. Further, she discusses the "magical forms in poetry," comparing the response a poem elicits in the reader to autistic children "mistaking the word for the thing" (p. 22).

Further, Atwood turns to the oral nature of poetry, as distinct from reading poetry aloud: "I would like the reader to be hearing it as a voice also" (Ingersoll, 1990, p. 23). Atwood notes how her poetry first comes to her, as images—here offering a key point we want to offer our students. Like most poets, Atwood cares more about the images than the ideas of poetry, the concrete over the abstract. By the end of the interview, Atwood discusses her use of parentheses, again a valuable idea for our class. She shows that the use of punctuation is a writer's purposeful choice and that punctuation impacts meaning—in Atwood's poetry, usually her working with two ideas at once.

When responding to Sandler's questions about critical reviews of Atwood's poetry, Atwood explains that the writing of her poems fall along a spectrum of highly crafted poems that are hard to write to poems that come fully formed: "The same with 'Threes.' I wrote it down and that was it" (Ingersoll, 1990, p. 49). For our students, we often portray serious poetry and all writing as monolithic, both the poem itself and the writing process. The truth, the reality, as Atwood expresses, is that some writing is highly crafted and some writing, especially poetry, can be both effective and essentially spontaneous. While producing a piece that is not revised much or at all is less likely with our students than professional writers, we have to be prepared to accept that some works can come to writers fully formed, if we are embracing authentic writing processes in our classes.

Atwood also offers an interesting "difference between conceiving a poem and conceiving a novel":

> A poem is something you hear, and the primary focus of interest is words. A novel is something you see, and the primary focus of interest is people. (Ingersoll, 1990, p. 50)

This interesting distinction is discounted immediately by Atwood, who then argues that poets write poetry because that is what poets do. She is leery of looking too closely at the writing process of poetry, although she adds, "[Y]ou can't write poetry unless you're willing to immerse yourself in language—not just in words, but in words of a certain potency" (p. 50). This view of poetry by Atwood confirms the value of spending extended time in our classes with students reading and writing poetry—not just with poetry as a goal, but with "words of a certain potency" as a goal.

Two interviews from 1978 by Joyce Carol Oates (Ingersoll, 1990) offer wonderful insight into Atwood's view of both poetry and how we teach poetry. Atwood discusses her interest in "words or phrases which appeal more because of their sound than their meaning, and the movement and phrasing of a poem are very important to me" (p. 69). Then she discusses the "texture of sound" in poetry and the tendency in her and other modern poets to prefer internal rhyme to end rhyme and "to avoid immediate alliteration and assonance in favor of echoes placed later in the poems" (p. 69). These highly specific comments are followed by Atwood's annoyance at students being steered toward the meaning in poetry by their teachers. She compares the search for meaning in our classes to "a prize out of a box of Cracker Jack" (p. 69).

Further into this interview Oates (Ingersoll, 1990) and Atwood discuss an assumption I listed above—"[T]he habit that presumably intelligent readers have of assuming that most writing, especially that in the first person, is autobiographical" (p. 71). Atwood muses about this habit, along with expressing her irritation for that assumption. First, she thinks that really effective writing might appear to be so real that readers want it to be literally true. Next, she explains that North Americans see a strong link between that which is written and the writer: "We think of 'writing' not as something you do but something you are" (p. 72). While Atwood rejects this obsession with writing being autobiographical, she does concede her own need to visit the actual places of her settings.

Toward the end of one interview by Oates (Ingersoll, 1990), Atwood discusses another assumption—that writers are disproportionately psychotic, that writing comes from artistic psychosis. Her argument is "that art, the making or creating, is done in spite of the neurosis, is a triumph over it" (p. 73). From the power of writing Atwood then moves to Oates's question about why Atwood writes; again, in typical Atwood style, Atwood rejects that narrow question and poses her own: "I think the real question is, 'Why doesn't everyone?'" (p. 73).

In the second interview by Oates (Ingersoll, 1990), Atwood returns to similar points she has made in the first interview. One interesting discussion, however, is Atwood addressing her writing schedule. As I noted above, Atwood is skeptical of process writing—a contrast to the field of writing instruction—and in this interview, Atwood's explanation of her writing schedule reveals her own proclivity toward procrastination and her own insecurities: "The fact is that blank pages inspire me with terror" (p. 79). Atwood offers our students a realistic view of how a writer writes—a view that rejects how we often characterize writing in school.

More directly discussing poetry, Fitz Gerald and Crabbe (Ingersoll, 1990) prompt Atwood to discuss poetic forms. Again, more as a writer than as a teacher, Atwood sounds exasperated: "I've never quite understood what 'free verse' was. It doesn't seem to me that any verse is entirely 'free'" (p. 133). She recognizes that such terms are ultimately inauthentic and inadequate. Ultimately, all poetry has structure, she seems to argue, although students of poetry, novices, "have not been taught to look for it," except in traditional forms such as meter and rhyme (p. 133). Here, she does support having students write formal forms, such as sonnets, although she rejects the emphasis we place on process and argues that formal education "doesn't help in *writing good poems*" (p. 134). Atwood feels that "[p]oets are largely self-taught" (p. 134), echoing Kurt Vonnegut's argument that we can't teach writing (Thomas, 2006).

Of Hooks and Eyes—The Poems of Margaret Atwood

The "hook and eye" is a type of fastener for clothing, often found on the traditional bra closure that consists of three or four hooks and the same number eyelets. Margaret Atwood depends on the reference in the opening stanza to her small poem:

you fit into me
like a hook into an eye.

If the reader makes the clothing fastener connection, Atwood's second and final stanza achieves the impact she desires:

> a fish hook
> an open eye.

We as readers flinch, possibly even covering our eyes and gasping. I know I have had whole classrooms of students moan.

The experiences I have had as a teacher of poetry with students' responding to Atwood's "you fit into me" are why I strongly suggest that we add many of her poems to our classrooms. She plays with words and ideas in ways that challenge her readers, and our students need to be challenged. Here, we will explore several of Atwood's poems, including her interests in nature and animals, in photography and mirrors, in war, and in language and perspectives. Much of the techniques and themes we find in Atwood's novels surface in her poetry as well, but with the intensity of language she associates with poetry—"words of a certain potency" (Ingersoll, 1990, p. 50).

About "This Is a Photograph of Me," Stein (1999) states that Atwood "challenges the reader to find the speaker drowned in the center" (p. 17). This poem incorporates elements commonly found in Atwood—photography, reflections, distortions of perspectives, nature. The photograph of the poem is itself distorted, "smeared" and "blurred" (11. 3, 4). After describing the scene of the photograph, the speaker reveals "The photograph was taken / the day after I drowned" (11. 15–16). The reader is left to decipher the narration from the grave, the "distortion" "of water / on light" (11. 22, 21–22). This poem helps our students explore the ambiguity of imagery and voice, here the voice of a drowned speaker. Stein believes this hidden, drowned speaker "tell[s] us that women have become invisible in contemporary Western culture and ask[s] that society acknowledge them" (p. 17).

CONNECTIONS

Lead singer and lyricist for rock group REM, Michael Stipe, is also a serious photographer, resulting in several references to photography in his lyrics. In "Nightswimming," from *Automatic for the People,* the lyrics begin with a photograph on the dashboard of a car, reflecting the picture backward. This distorted image pairs well with Atwood's poem. In "Camera," from *Reckoning,* Stipe uses the camera as a metaphor: "If I'm to be your camera, then who will be your face?" Co-written with Nathalie Merchant, "Photograph" includes a photograph "found . . . / underneath the broken glass," again a distortion. These poems offer similar uses of imagery with Atwood, and song lyrics often resonate well with students, especially those who are not as likely to believe they are interested in poetry.

Atwood's "The Animals in that Country" asks the reader to note the distinction between "that country" (1. 1) and "this country" (1. 21), suggesting a commentary by the speaker. The poem's first twenty lines address the "ceremonial" (1. 3) and the mythic through fox hunts, bullfights, and legends of werewolves. These romanticized views of the destruction of animals in "that country," where "animals/have the faces of people" (11. 1–2), is contrasted with "this country," where "animals/have the faces of/animals" (11. 21–23). In "this country," animals die in the headlights of careless cars: "Their deaths are not elegant" (1. 27). Mixing the mythic with reality, Atwood confronts how humans view and treat animals in this poem. Readers are left wondering whether there are two actual countries or simply two states of mind about animals—or both.

CONNECTIONS

Poet and outdoorsman James Dickey was associated with poetry about war, but he writes often about animals, hunting, and the tension between domesticity and wildness. My students responded well to Dickey's poetry, I have found. His "A Dog Sleeping on My Feet," "The Heaven of Animals," and "Deer Among Cattle" pair perfectly with Atwood's "The Animals in that Country." The speaker in "A Dog Sleeping on My Feet" becomes the dog while he sleeps, as the poem's title suggests, with the dog on his feet; this poem mixes fox hunting with the creative act of writing. Dickey imagines "The Heaven of Animals" in one of his most anthologized poems. This heaven celebrates the essence of animals, contrasting with the idealistic view of heaven for humans. In the heaven of animals the predator/prey cycle exists perfectly and perpetually. A wonderful image of domesticity and wildness is captured in "Deer among Cattle," which depicts the speaker finding in "the searing beam / Of my hand" (11. 1–2) a deer in a fenced cow pasture. The cattle are "bred- / for-slaughter" (11. 7–8), while the deer is free.

Atwood loves to play with language, and her poetry is possibly her favorite playground. In "Spelling," the speaker watches as her "daughter plays on the floor / with plastic letters" (11. 1–2), learning to spell as children do. That first stanza twists "how to spell" into "how to make spells," suggesting magic (11. 4, 6). This subtle message about the magic of language is expressed through Atwood's own ability to cast spells on her readers. This poem challenges students with a moment of their young lives that is possibly lost—learning the language through play. (John Dewey, the much renowned educator and philosopher, believed that students didn't need to learn to read because he couldn't remember learning it!) The second poem turns

dramatically in tone, musing about women who choose words over children; this is a political poem that confronts the tension women artists feel between their calling to be artists and their drives to be mothers (both biological and societal impulses). The poem turns darker and darker relating childbirth to war and drawing an image of a witch burned at the stake. By the end, the speaker confesses to be speaking in metaphor—much as Atwood does in "Tricks with Mirrors"—and forces the reader to consider the power of words and the power of naming. This poem is an excellent opportunity to discuss how poets raise political themes in common moments, here the gender conflicts of being an artist found in a child playing "with plastic letters" (1. 2).

The power of language and voice infused with mythic allusion drives Atwood's "Siren Song." This poem represents Atwood's interest both in mythic patterns and reframing those patterns. The speaker confesses early that "the song / . . . is irresistible" (11. 2–3). The allusion to mythical Sirens who lured sailors to their deaths unfolds in the first stanzas where the speaker confesses no one knows the Siren's song because "anyone who has heard it / is dead" (11. 8–9). By the forth stanza, the speaker becomes inviting and confesses her miserable existence. The seventh stanza promises a shared secret, if the reader will "Come closer" (1. 21). The tone grows to panic by the end—where readers discover that *we* are victims of the Siren's song: "it works every time" (1. 27).

"At the Tourist Center in Boston" echoes Atwood's portrayal of tourists found in her characterization of strangers, tourists, and foreigners in *Dancing Girls*. In this poem, which ends with three questions, the speaker considers "my country" as it is portrayed through a map and through advertising (1. 1). A central technique of the poem is Atwood's blossoming tone that grows from her sharp diction throughout the poem; students should be asked to look closely at that diction to explain how that creates the tone, how that expresses Atwood's attitude about her theme of the portrayal of Canada as that portrayal contrasts reality. In the first stanza, the map of Canada is "reduced" (p. 4), and by the fourth stanza, the speaker describes the advertisements with "grinning," "immaculate," "smokeless," and "teeth white as detergent" (11. 16, 21, 22). Stein (1999) explains that this poem "use[s] landscape to explore the cultural, economic, and political relations between Canada and the United States" (p. 20). The subtlety of this poem grows from the title—the speaker is in Boston and Canadian—but students often miss key information in titles.

"Now look objectively. You have to / admit the cancer cell is beautiful" opens Atwood's "Cell," a poem that finds poetry where students would least expect it (11. 1–2). Atwood has stated that her novels often come from a "What if?"; in this poem, the speaker forces the reader to rethink cancer as "[i]f it were a flower" (1. 3). The contrast of blossoming flowers and blossoming cancer asks the reader to reconsider both "beauty" and "objectivity." By the last stanza, the reader learns that cancer's beauty is *It has forgotten / how to die* (11. 19–20). Then the last stanza rattles off short "To" phrases that build to "Such desires / are not unknown. Look in the mirror" (11. 23–24). Cancer is *human* in its desire for immortality.

Just as the point of view in her fiction drives her themes, the speaker in her "The Loneliness of the Military Historian" gives Atwood's consideration of war texture and invites the reader to look at layers of attitudes toward war. The speaker contrasts herself with Medusa in the long opening stanza when she acknowledges the weight of her profession as military historian. The speaker seems to contrast her role as historian with being a "prophetess" (1. 8). But the second stanza complicates this consideration of war and of history by the speaker raising the issue of gender—"women should not contemplate war" and "Women should march for peace" (11. 16, 20). The third stanza turns away from sexual stereotypes and toward "what I hope will pass as truth" (1. 34). She mixes her pursuit of truth with objectivity (also explored in "Cell") and the role of writing history; in the next stanza, she contrasts the goals of the historian with the poet. The next stanza returns to her view of war and her commitment to description without judgment—"Despite the propaganda, there are no monsters" (1. 60). As dispassionate historian, she notes that God has abandoned many who fight in the name of God while "rats and cholera have won many wars" (1. 78). The military historian is a researcher, and her culminating point is mere "statistics: / for every year of peace there have been four hundred / years of war" (11. 104–106).

CONNECTIONS

"The Loneliness of the Military Historian" includes an historian's interest in war and her visiting battlefields. Many students, again, might miss the word "loneliness" in the title—which seems to show the historian is somehow alienated by her focus on war; as well, students often miss the tone of poems that address war. Mainstream culture tends to be patriotic, tends to support its own wars, while poets almost invariably reject war by painting its horrors. William Stafford's "At the Un-national Monument along the Canadian Border" shares with Atwood her use of Canada as a contrast to the U.S. as well as including the key detail of Canada in the title. Further, Stafford's poem evokes an objective tone similar to Atwood's poem, both of which depend on a perceptive reader to infer their themes rejecting the glorification of war. The historian in Atwood's poem helps perpetuate our celebrating war while Stafford mocks that celebration through his poem's ironic praise of peace by never mentioning the words but acknowledging "that people celebrate it by forgetting its name" (1. 10).

- -

Atwood and Stafford show us that history, what we remember, is what we write down—all else can be forgotten. Yet, what we write down becomes *one version* of the truth, as Atwood reminds us again and again. "Half-Hanged Mary" gives the historical Mary Webster (noted in the dedication of Atwood's *The Handmaid's Tale*), who survived her hanging for being a witch in the 1680s, a voice for her ordeal. The poem is structured by sections that chronicle the time that passes during Mary's hanging from 7 P.M. until later than 8 A.M. the next morning. The poem covers several pages so it is an excellent opportunity to have students study a longer poem that is accessible, interesting, and challenging. Since the poem is long, I'll list some ideas here by sections, but the poem deserves a significant time to study:

- 7 P.M.—This section confronts the reader with the hanging and the circumstances that make Mary "guilty," "for living alone" and "breasts" (11. 10, 15).
- 8 P.M.—Here, Mary reveals the nastiness of the hanging and the hatred driving the men who do the hanging.
- 9 P.M.—The women who watch in this section contrast with the men who hang Mary, fear against hatred. Along with the tension of Mary's connection with her executioners, Atwood begins to infuse the voice of Mary with wordplay, "Birds / of a feather burn together" (11. 14–15).
- 10 P.M.—The wordplay continues as Mary addresses God directly. Students should be asked to address the tone of this section.
- 12 midnight—As the night turns toward morning, Mary struggles against death in this section where death is alluring as an escape.
- 2 A.M.—Mary turns to prayer; this section can be compared with the tone in the 10 P.M. section where she is abrupt with God.
- 3 A.M.—Punctuation disappears in this section as Mary slips into a delusional state. Students can be asked to consider how Atwood manipulates punctuation (or its absence) for meaning in this section.
- 6 A.M.—The sunrise of the morning is triumphant for Mary who is "[a]t the end of my rope" but who "will have two" deaths (11. 159, 163).
- 8 A.M.—The shock of her survival becomes ironic, as Mary announces that her living through the hanging transforms her: "Before I was not a witch. / But now I am one" (11. 182–183).
- Later—The triumphant final section represents a key theme of

Atwood's work—the power of language. "The words boil out of me," she exclaims (1. 211).

- -
CONNECTION

The Handmaid's Tale is a direct connection with "Half-Hanged Mary" since Atwood dedicates the book to Mary Webster. Further, we can ask students to research the historical Mary Webster, which should help students see that we marginalize women in historical accounts.

- -

Several of Atwood's poems in *Morning in the Burned House* address her father—"A Pink Hotel in California," "A Visit," and "Bored." Triggered by furniture in a pink hotel room, memories of the speaker's father flood her mind in "A Pink Hotel in California." This poem is an excellent model for students to write about their own family member, focusing on specific memories as Atwood does. This poem looks at flashback; her memories of her father in 1943 spurred by "the chest of drawers / [that] has antique man-bored wormholes" (11. 31–32) come to her in 1994. The opening stanza of "A Visit" turns from memories of her father to the realization of his infirmary:

> Gone are the days
> When you could walk on water.
> When you could walk. (11. 1–3)

The allusion to Jesus infuses the poem with the stark reality that children must face concerning the mortality of their parents. "Bored" is certainly a poem students can relate to since the speaker of this poem looks back at her boredom during her childhood, a boredom she sees differently as an adult. The speaker by the end of the poem sees the "minutiae" differently (1. 24): "Why do I remember it as sunnier / all the time then . . . ?" (11. 30–31). The speaker realizes she "wouldn't be bored" if she could have these times back (1. 37).

- -
CONNECTIONS

Poets look closely at family relationships. Sharon Olds's *The Father* offers disorienting and stark explorations of Olds's relationship with her father during his illness, the irony of her care for him despite his disregard for her. A memory sparked similarly to the scene in "A Pink Hotel in California" is the focus of Li-Young Lee's "The Gift." This poem shares some elements with Atwood, such as looking backward and at a moment in front of the speaker. These poems read together show students the complexities of parent-child relationships as well as the nuances of poetic expression. Further, students might find these poems inspiration for their own poetry about a parent or other family connections.

The speaker of "The Moment" raises an interesting conflict between the human concept of ownership and the natural world's response. The first stanza connects "hard work and a long voyage" with the possessions we accumulate (1. 2). But in the second stanza the natural world stands up to the claim. The final stanza gives the natural world a voice, a common technique by Atwood: "*No, they whisper. You own nothing*" (1. 13). The final stanza confronts the reader and the assumptions about ownership common to Western thinking. The response of the natural world also goes beyond the illusion of ownership and rejects the concept of discovery: "*You never found us / It was always the other way around*" (11. 17–18).

CONNECTIONS

Many of our students take possessions for granted along with few having ever questioned the value or fact of ownership. Two essays by Barbara Kingsolver would match Atwood's "The Moment" well—"Making Peace" and "The Spaces Between." Asking students to rethink their capitalistic assumptions about owning objects is challenging. In these works, the contrast of ownership with nature adds another element to the theme of ownership, a theme that confronts Western thinking.

The first line—"In the burned house I am eating breakfast"—of "Morning in the Burned House" immediately disorients the reader. Stein (1999) explains that the poem "is built . . . on paradoxes of memory and the passage of time. For we experience our memories, our stories, as if they are real" (p. 124). The poem asks the reader to consider if the burned house is real or a metaphor for loss. The details of the poem evoke a wide range of the senses as the speaker investigates the ruins that are also memories, "every detail clear" (1. 13). The mix of loss and destruction with vivid memories is disturbing and somehow inviting. The poem ends with similar contrasts: "my cindery, non-existent, / radiant flesh. Incandescent" (11. 35–36).

The poetry of Atwood is challenging and confrontational in the themes, the topics, and the poetry. They are perfect for our classes where we want students to be disoriented by language and inspired by language. "Nothing like love to put blood / back in the language," Atwood writes in "Nothing"; nothing like Atwood's poetry to put blood back into our classrooms, our students.

Risking Poetry with Atwood— Students as Poets

Similar to my comments in Chapter Six about asking students to write short fiction is my belief that we must approach assigning the writing of poetry with more rigor—or simply stop asking students to write poetry. As we are reading and discussing Atwood's poetry, we should be in constant pursuit of answering a central question: What makes poetry *poetry*? Trying to answer that question improves our students as readers—and thinkers—but it also provides them a framework for drafting and composing poetry themselves. I have begun to consider how difficult asking students to write poetry is when compared to other writing assignments; as I noted in the last chapter, writing short fiction is a challenging writing assignment. Heard (1999) argues that poetry is well within the reach of *all* students, regardless of age or ability. I have begun to agree.

Yet, my experience with high school and college students shows that they often produce both poetry and short fiction that is flawed by their own assumptions and by their experiences with these forms throughout their schooling. Yes—even with poetry, we must assign, teach, and assess with the same rigor as with any writing assignment, as I discussed in Chapter Six. I recommend that the writing of poetry can be successful and even a pivotal writing experience in our classes if we use the following guiding principles:

- While students read Atwood, we must ask them to look closely at the key distinguishing factor in poetry—purposeful formation of lines and stanzas. Prose is driven by sentence and paragraph formation while poetry is primarily unique for its use of lines and stanzas as its form. Poetry and prose share all other craft elements such as figurative language, voice, rhythm, and even rhyme. A primary focus of our feedback and assessment of original student poetry, then, must address the *purposeful* formation of lines and stanzas.

- Students asked to write poetry write better poetry if they are asked to work through some writing exercises targeted on poetic principles. Here is where we can implement the practice of having students try traditional forms such as sonnets, couplets, blank verse, syllabic verse, and other forms that ask students to conform to structure and conventional expectations. I prefer to see these as writing exercises, not as authentic poetry—although students often will explore these traditional forms further on their own when asked to write original poetry.

- When students are asked to draft original poems, I give them strict parameters as I do with writing short stories. One restriction is to ask students to draft at least three poems; from those poems, they should ultimately choose *one* to submit. (This is a concept endorsed often by James Dickey when he advised young poets about how to know what poems to submit for publication.) Another restriction is to ban students from using rhyme; this restriction forces students to explore other craft elements that produce poetic language—rich use of figurative language, conscious orchestration of rhythm (even meter), an emphasis on sound devices. As well, I give them a minimum line requirement; twelve or fourteen lines are generally enough to encourage them to explore line and stanza formation.

- Poetry lends itself to being heard. Students should be encouraged to read their poems aloud as part of their drafting and to read their poems aloud for classmates. Many feel that poetry *must* be heard, although many modern and contemporary poets are more concerned about how the words look on the page. Especially during the composing of poetry, a discussion about the value of the sound of poetry and the look of poetry can help our students develop in their purposefulness as writers.

The writing of poetry will not create a classroom of poets in any of our classes, but the writing of poetry will help our students grow as readers, writers, and thinkers—especially if we treat our poetry writing assignments with the respect they deserve, the respect Atwood shows her readers in the craft of her poetry.

ENTRY POINTS AND CONNECTIONS

"Ars Poetica," Archibald MacLeish

"Poetry," Marianne Moore

"Nightswimming," "Camera," REM

"Photograph," Natalie Merchant and Michael Stipe

"A Dog Sleeping on My Feet," "The Heaven on Animals," "Deer Among Cattle," James Dickey

"At the Un-national Monument along the Canadian Border," William Stafford

The Handmaid's Tale, Margaret Atwood

The Father, Sharon Olds

"The Gift," Li-Young Lee

"Diving into the Wreck," Adrienne Rich

Chapter Eight

Children and Wordplay

Expanding Our Views of Literature

What's this about Chicken Little? It appears "Chicken Little read too many news papers. He listened to the radio too much, and he watched too much television. One day something snapped," explains Atwood (2006) in her "Chicken Little Goes Too Far" from *The Tent*. Atwood returns to her interest in fables, this time a children's story. But as we might expect, Atwood's rendition of Chicken Little isn't the story we recall. In Atwood's version, the tale becomes an allegory and satire of today.

Chicken Little shouts his "The sky is falling!" first to Henny Penny, "who was loading groceries into her four-wheel-drive super-van" (p. 67). Now a soccer mom, Henny Penny shrugs off Chicken Little although he explains that his cry "is a metaphor" (p. 68). Next, Chicken Little makes his plea to Turkey Lurkey, a scathing satire of university professors. "That's one analysis," Turkey Lurkey replies to Chicken Little. "But there's data to show it isn't that sky that's falling" (p. 68). Turkey Lurkey explains that the earth is rising. When Chicken Little argues that such an analysis is irrelevant since the results are the same, Turkey Lurkey calls Chicken Little "simple minded . . . with offensive condescension" (p. 69). Atwood's parody of the arrogant intellectual elite here reminds readers of her "Historical Notes" in *The Handmaid's Tale.*

Goosey Loosey, a newspaper editor and friend of Chicken Little, refuses to report on Chicken Little's claim because "The sky is falling!" does not compare with "'The stock market is falling,'" adding a sharp cut at both journalism and capitalism (p. 69). This sends Chicken Little to the bar where the bartender, Skunky Punky, shows the same disdain for Chicken Little's cry as all the rest. But this trip leads Ducky Lucky to overhearing Chicken Little and offering his lobbying services—for a fee. Uninterested in paying, Chicken Little is inspired to form his own campaign, complete with an acronym (TSIF for The Sky Is Falling), a website, and picketing!

When Chicken Little attracts a following and appears to be making a difference, Hoggy Groggy, a developer of retirement communities, seeks the services of Foxy Loxy. A hitman, Foxy Loxy takes the job with a simple, "I eat guys like that for breakfast" (p. 71). And the tale ends with Foxy Loxy asking what he will be paid; Hoggy Groggy says, with the wordplay common in Atwood, "The sky's the limit"; the reader learns, "And so it was" (p. 71). A dark tale with a bitter moral to the story.

This is the stuff of Atwood we will look at briefly in Chapter Eight—Atwood's wordplay, her books for children, and her writing that can add joy and value to our classrooms. It seems to me that after the first few grades of school, the fun of language is left behind as if it has no academic value. But, we all enjoy wordplay, humor, and satire; we all manipulate language to elicit laughter and shock. These joyous moments with language are not just breaks from the serious work in our classes, however. They are essential to what we do with language.

Tales Retold—Atwood's *The Tent*

Literature is literature. But in school, we make clear distinctions and judgments that relegate some literature here and some literature there. We have children's literature, young adult literature, and *literature*. Most of us see children's literature as a necessary first experience with literature, although some remain skeptical of the growing picture book market; if Dr. Seuss and Shel Silverstein were good enough for me, then they are good enough for everyone, some claim. Then there is young adult literature. A much more troubling topic. Many reject YA lit outright, others see it as a way to hook students on reading before pushing them on to *real* literature, and a few souls embrace YA lit as *real* literature.

In this chapter, I am arguing for an opening of the canon, an expanding of how we see literature and how we choose literature for our classes. We can bring literature written for any age into our classrooms and investigate or re-investigate what we all think and assume about literature and the conventions of these forms. As well, I believe these experiences with literature are the perfect opportunities to infuse our classes with humor, joy, and wordplay.

Three other pieces from *The Tent* are excellent works that play on conventions of children's literature and fables (as we saw in "Chicken Little Goes Too Far") allowing us opportunities to discuss how our students view children's literature before bringing some of Atwood's picture books into our classes along with other children's literature—"Winter's Tales," "The Animals Reject Their Names and Things Return to Their Origins," and "King Log in Exile." Each of these pieces works through and against conventional aspects of children's literature—"once upon a time," heavy rhyme and sound devices, narrative verse, morals, direct references to words and literary technique.

CONNECTION

Many writers bring their love for language and wordplay into their own works by manipulating and retelling classic fables, myths, and legends. John Gardner, known for his *Grendel* (a retelling of the *Beowulf* legend from the viewpoint of the monster), has a collection of short fiction that pairs well with Atwood's *The Tent* as a work playing with tales—*The King's Indian: Stories and Tales*. Like Atwood, Gardner's stories are ripe with conventional aspects of tales while also being highly satiric. Both Gardner and Atwood challenge students in terms of their background knowledge and their sensitivity to tone and parody.

"Winter's Tales" is a perfect opening piece when we are exploring children's literature since the tale begins, "Once upon a time" (p. 43). However, once Atwood establishes our expectations of a classic tale perhaps similar to Cinderella, her story shifts quickly to the horrific that we somehow often ignore in fables and tales: "[T]here were germs with horns" (p. 43). Those germs can be killed by bleach, we learn, and "[y]ou could commit suicide by drinking this bleach, and some women did" (p. 43)—a frightful opening paragraph that may not be suitable for children. Yet, we can use this opening paragraph to discuss the conventional opening and to brainstorm a class of students' knowledge of children's stories. Further, we can bring in classic children's stories, fables, and tales to look carefully at the dark elements found in most of them—from Little Red Riding Hood to *Alice in Wonderland*.

By the second paragraph, we realize this is an older person speaking about and to the young, thus Winter's Tales. "Once upon a time" in the second paragraph now carries a tone of disdain by the older speaker for youth. The third paragraph reinvents the "good old days," but this version isn't so good since in that "once upon a time,"

"There were no telephones, there were no vaccinations; so you couldn't call the doctor when you were dying" (pp. 43–44). The tale continues with a dim view of the past, especially for women. "All of these were metaphors for unsatisfactory sex," the narrator explains about women's lives (p. 44).

The tale ends with a discussion of meat loaf and pot roast, told as if the narrator is revealing a secret charm. The great regret of this tale is that the young probably aren't listening because "that's what they want—war stories, and disgusting menus. They want suffering, they want scars" (p. 45). As a tale, this story offers our students conventional story patterns along with a bitter view of the "good old days"; Atwood's tale is driven by narration, convention, and a feminist eye.

In Kurt Vonnegut's *Slaughterhouse-Five,* one unforgettable motif is the playing of a war movie backwards, everything scrambling backward toward peace. In the long poem, "The Animals Reject Their Names and Things Return to Their Origins," Atwood sends everything back to the very beginning from a simple idea—a bear rejects the names placed upon it by humans. After rejecting all names for the bear in the first stanza, the bear adds, "Forget fairy tales, in which I was / your shaggy puppet, prince in hairshirt, surrogate / for human demons" (11. 11–13). Further, the bear also "renounce[s] metaphor" (1. 20). Language and story are central elements of this poem that looks at the power of naming and the power of speaking against the oppression of words.

The bear instead embraces its growl, and in the second section, "the dictionaries began to untwist, / and time stalled and reversed" (11. 38–39). The rest of the poem is a brilliant depiction of the untwisting of the world—a list of things reversing. We watch as mice are flung back out of traps (mice are favorites in fairy tales and children's stories) and flowers slip back into being buds. As the world reverses itself in wonderful and perceptive ways (Atwood's choices are all loaded), section three sends humanity back to the first human, Adam, and shows humanity "alone at the first naming"— where human perversions of "*dominion*" is noted along with Adam "deprived/of his arsenal of proper nouns/return[ing] to mud" (11. 92, 95, 97–99).

The fourth section explains, "I could end this with a moral / as if this were a fable about animals / though no fables are really about animals" (11. 107–109). These lines are perfect for our classrooms and our discussions of fables. Children's literature, like all literature, deals with multiple levels—one level implying one or more other levels. While high school and college students may be able to see those levels more easily in children's stories, I feel that does not suggest that children's literature is lower than other literature. The poem ends with a wry rejection of morals, though, because now readers "can't read this / because you can't remember the word for *read*" (11. 118–119).

"King Log in Exile" echoes "The Frog King" from the *Brothers Grimm's Fairy Tales.* Atwood's version reveals itself as a tale that parodies political leaders. King Log is "deposed by the frogs" for King Stork (p. 121). Immediately after the change of power, King Stork eats "his new subjects," much to their chagrin (p. 121). King Log believes he has done nothing wrong, but he soon realizes, "He had done—in a word—nothing" (p. 122). He failed the frogs by being weak, but we learn he had sat passively by as "[t]here had been a sharp upturn in exports, the chief commodity being frogs' legs" (p. 122). The truth appears to be that King Log reaps financial benefits while *others* slaughter the frogs—a small detail and little difference from the actions of King Stork. This tale ends with King Log, who "let the rot set in" while king, "sprouting a fine crop of shitake mushrooms" and writing his memoirs; the Stork King eats all his subjects, sells "the tadpoles into sexual slavery," and prepares the drained pond for "desirable residential estates" (p. 123). Moral: Political leaders weak and strong benefit always while those who choose them suffer. Atwood offers a fitting tale for any time and any people, it would seem.

CONNECTIONS

Both fairy tales from the Brothers Grimm and Aesop's Fables are suitable companions to these tales by Atwood. Our students can enjoy rereading these works, discovering tales and fables they have never read, and even reading the original tales for the first time. Since these works pre-date copyright laws, they are all accessible through the Internet, making a unit studying these tales and fables an interesting and revealing activity for any students.

Myth patterns, fables, and legends run throughout most of Atwood's works regardless of genre. In *The Tent,* she offers our students brief pieces that explore conventions of fables and tales along with elements commonly found in children's literature. Now let's turn to Atwood's literature written specifically for children, works that our students can enjoy as well.

Picture Books and Children's Literature— Atwood for All Ages

Atwood was known early in her life and career as an artist and a poet. She drew and published her own cartoons that show her scathing wit and wordplay far before she received recognition for her novels. *Up in the Tree* (1978) was a children's book that Atwood wrote, illustrated, and hand-lettered. Filled with simple colors—red, blue, and brown— and simple words, the story is filled with rhyme and repetition that we associate with children's books such as those by Dr. Seuss. The two children, a girl and a boy who look quite similar, play in a tree, where "[t]here's nothing to fear," until their ladder is taken by beavers. Stranded, the children panic, but a bird comes to their rescue. When they return to the ground, they build stairs back into the tree. The final page is the children wrapped in blankets sleeping in the tree.

This would be a great entry into asking our students to write, illustrate, and letter a small book of their own. Making a book is something we ask elementary students to do often, but as children get older, this wonderfully fulfilling act is left out of our classes. Book making can be of two kinds with our high school and college students. Of course, the technology-savvy students will want to write and create a book electronically. While the software and computers available for this activity are inviting, I would recommend the second option— asking students to write and create a book by hand, much as Atwood did.

ENTRY POINT

One of the best activities I ever did with my students involved listening to and then writing children's stories for elementary classes. My high school students loved a reading of Rudyard Kipling's "Elephant's Child" by Jack Nicholson with the music provided by Bobby McFerrin. After listening to this story and talking about characteristics of children's stories, I would put my high school students in small groups to write their own children's stories that we would take to read to elementary classes. Originally, I used this activity to prepare students for writing their own short stories; now I see that we should spend more time taking the children's story as seriously as we did their short stories.

Atwood did not return to writing for children until she published a chapter book titled *For the Birds* in 1990; it is illustrated by John Bianchi and includes factual information by Shelley Tanaka. This book could be combined with the book-making activity above as *For the Birds* adds a multi-genre element to her first book. In this chapter book, Atwood writes a fictional narrative, with Tanaka providing factual information in side-bars. As well, Atwood models using her personal and political interests as a part of her whole persona, writing a book that has a conscience and an educational purpose.

More recently, Atwood has written three picture books—*Princess Prunella and the Purple Peanut* (1995), *Rude Ramsay and the Roaring Radishes* (2003), and *Bashful Bob and Doleful Dorinda* (2006). As the titles reveal, this is Atwood playing with words at her best. These works are tours de force in alliteration and the conventional expectations of children's stories. *Princess Prunella and the Purple Peanut* plays with the letter "p," of course, but it also works within the princess motif we know in many classic tales and fables. Mixed into these classic motifs is a modern or even postmodern sensibility and tone; the parents are pinheaded, for example. Beyond the relentless use of alliteration, this book asks students to consider diction and tone—particularly in terms of appropriateness for children. This first picture book by Atwood shares its biting tone with writers such as Shel Silverstein. As many of our students will know too well, sarcasm by children is often not well received. Here, we can discuss the nature of tone and children, something they have probably not addressed before.

Rude Ramsay and the Roaring Radishes and *Bashful Bob and Doleful Dorinda* share an illustrator, Dusan Petricic, and these picture books are excellent ways to have students consider both the writing and the illustrations as elements of the story. One aspect of children's literature often omitted in adult literature (if there is such a thing) is illustrations. Cartoons, comic books, and graphic novels are often relegated to children. Many adults, however, love these forms, and many cartoons ostensibly for children are equally appropriate for adults. Our students should consider how illustrations contribute to both meaning and tone in these picture books—as they do in the cartoons, comics, and graphic novels they read outside of class.

Children's stories, modern or classic, are comic and dark—just like life. And the best literature, regardless of its intended audience's age, deserves reading and rereading, particularly as the reader grows and necessarily changes. Playing with words is also something we should do throughout our lives, especially in our classrooms. Atwood is brilliant regardless of genre, regardless of the accompanying illustrations.

Entry Points and Connections

The King's Indian: Stories and Tales, John Gardner

Brothers Grimm's Fairy Tales (available at www.cs.cmu.edu/~spok/grimmtmp/)

Aesop's Fables (available at www.aesopfables.com)

"Elephant's Child," Rudyard Kipling

A Community for Reading, Writing, Learning

Writing of her vocation as a writer in *Writing with Intent*, Atwood (2005) offers, "Either way, you're part of a community, the community of writers, the community of storytellers that stretches back through time to the beginning of human society" (p. 108). She lives, walks, and writes the life of a writer. It is a life we want to bring into the community of learners in our classrooms.

Atwood represents for me what this series hopes to accomplish because she confronts her readers on many levels. Her works span virtually every genre and medium; she infuses her works with mythological motifs that re-vision both those classic motifs and contemporary themes. Atwood as a writer also defies simple definitions for female writers, for feminist writers.

From her writings to her interviews, Atwood speaks with a political and artistic conviction that grows from her commitment to being both. But if you read *The Handmaid's Tale* closely, her portrayal of Offred/June's mother, her connecting Offred/June to violent urges, her "Historical Notes"—all offer the reader more questions than answers. Atwood as an artist who is often political does not stoop to ideological rants in her works, but she confronts those things she finds troubling.

When my students read *The Handmaid's Tale,* "Rape Fantasies," or her brief poem "you fit into me," we found ourselves energized and having discussions that were rarely matched by discussions of any other works. Atwood confronts, but she also inspires us to think.

"But few succumb to temptations they find unattractive," Atwood (2005) explains in *Writing with Intent*. "What is it, this compulsion to scrawl things on blank pages? Why this boundless out-flowing of words? What drives us to it? Is writing some sort of disease? Or rather—being speech in visual form—is it simply a manifestation of being human? I choose the latter" (p. 188). And I believe bringing Atwood into our classrooms will instill a compulsion both to read and to write in our students—and us.

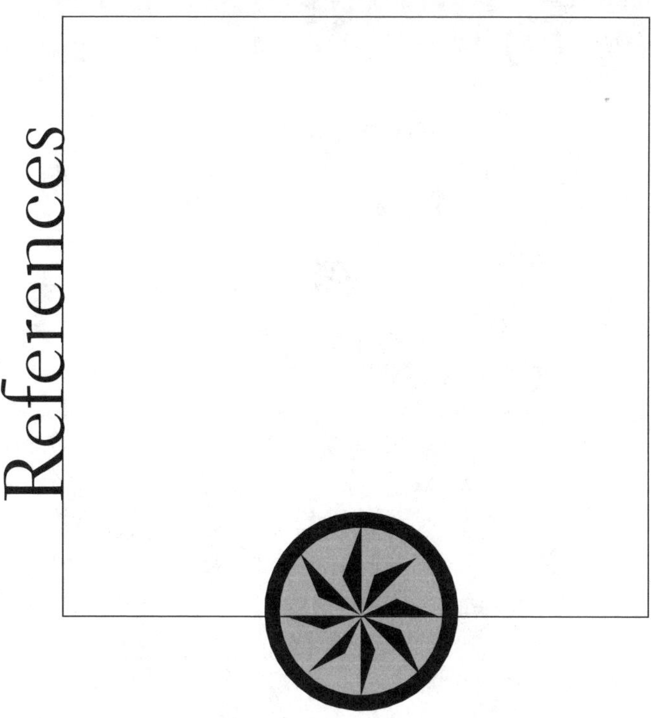

References

Atwood, M. (1996/1997). *Alias Grace*. New York: Anchor.

Atwood, M. (2006). *Bashful Bob and Doleful Dorinda*. New York: Bloomsbury Children's Books.

Atwood, M. (2000/2001). *The blind assassin*. New York: Anchor.

Atwood, M. (1983/1998). *Bluebeard's egg*. New York: Anchor.

Atwood, M. (1981/1998). *Bodily harm*. New York: Anchor.

Atwood, M. (1989/1998). *Cat's eye*. New York: Anchor.

Atwood, M. (1977/1998). *Dancing girls*. New York: Anchor.

Atwood, M. (1998). *Eating fire: Selected poetry 1965–1995*. London: Virago.

Atwood, M. (1969/1998). *The edible woman*. New York: Anchor.

Atwood, M. (1990). *For the birds*. Toronto: Douglas and McIntyre.

Atwood, M. (1985/1998). *The handmaid's tale*. New York: Anchor.

Atwood, M. (1976/1998). *Lady oracle*. New York: Anchor.

Atwood, M. (1979/1998). *Life before man*. New York: Anchor.

Atwood, M. (2006). *Moral disorder: And other stories*. New York: Nan A. Talese.

Atwood, M. (1995). *Morning in the burned house*. Boston: Houghton Mifflin.

Atwood, M. (2002). *Negotiating with the dead: A writer on writing*. New York: Anchor Books.

Atwood, M. (2003/2004). *Oryx and Crake*. New York: Anchor.

Atwood, M. (2005/2006). *The Penelopiad*. London: Canongate U. S.

Atwood, M. (1995). *Princess Prunella and the purple peanut*. New York: Workman.

Atwood, M. (1993/1998). *The robber bride*. New York: Anchor.

Atwood, M. (2003). *Rude Ramsay and the roaring radishes*. New York: Bloomsbury Children's.

Atwood, M. (1982). *Second words*. Boston: Beacon.

Atwood, M. (1972/1998). *Surfacing*. New York: Anchor.

Atwood, M. (2006). *The tent*. New York: Nan A. Talese.

Atwood, M. (1978/2006). *Up in the tree*. Toronto: Groundwood.

Atwood, M. (1995, June). Waterstone's poetry lecture. Retrieved July 12, 2006, from: http://www.library.utoronto.ca/canpoetry/atwood/write.htm.

Atwood, M. (1991/1998). *Wilderness tips*. New York: Anchor.

Atwood, M. (2005). *Writing with intent: Essays, reviews, personal prose: 1983–2005*. New York: Carroll and Graf.

Bloom, H. (1994). *The western canon: The books and school of the ages*. New York: Harcourt, Brace.

Campbell, J., & Moyers, B. (1988). *The power of myth*. New York: Doubleday.

Cooke, N. (1998). *Margaret Atwood: A biography*. Toronto: ECW.

Cooke, N. (2004). *Margaret Atwood: A critical companion*. Westport, CT: Greenwood.

Darton, J. (2001). *Writers on writing: Collected essays from* The New York Times. New York: Times Books.

DeSalvo, L. (1996). *Vertigo: A memoir*. New York: Dutton.

Dickey, J. (1967). *James Dickey: Poems 1957–1967*. Middleton, CT: Wesleyan University Press.

Farr, J. (1992). *The passion of Emily Dickinson*. Cambridge, MA: Harvard University Press.

Freire, P. (1993). *Pedagogy of the oppressed*. New York: Continuum.

Gardner, H. (2000). *The disciplined mind: Beyond facts and standardized tests, the K–12 education that every child deserves*. New York: Penguin.

Gardner, J. (1991). *The art of fiction: Notes on craft for young writers*. New York: Vintage.

Gardner, J. (1974). *The king's Indian: Stories and tales*. New York: Ballantine.

Gardner, J. (1978). *On moral fiction*. New York: Basic.

Gardner, J. (1999). *On becoming a novelist*. New York: W. W. Norton.

Greene, M. (1995). *Releasing the imagination: Essays on education, the arts, and social change*. San Francisco: Jossey-Bass.

Hand, E. (2005, December 25). The new muses. *The Washington Post*.

Heard, G. (1999). *Awakening the heart: Exploring poetry in elementary and middle school*. Portsmouth, NH: Heinemann.

Howells, C. A. (1995). *Modern novelists: Margaret Atwood*. New York: St. Martin's Press.

Ingersoll, E. G., ed. (1990). *Margaret Atwood: Conversations*. Princeton, NJ: Ontario Review.

Jaeger, E. (2006, Spring). Silencing teachers in an era of scripted reading. *Rethinking Schools, 20* (3), 39–41.

Kafka, F. (1979). *The basic Kafka*. New York: Pocket.

Kingsolver, B. (1998). *Another America: Otra America*. Trans. Rebecca Cartes. New York: Seal.

Kohn, A. (2006, March). The trouble with rubrics. *English Journal, 95* (4), 12–15.

Myers, B. (2004, December). How poems work: Gwendolyn MacEwen, "Dark pines under water." *Arc Poetry Magazine*. Retrieved September 26, 2006, at: http://www.arcpoetry.ca/howpoemswork/features/2004_12_myers.php.

Nischik, R. M., ed. (2000). *Margaret Atwood: Works and impact*. Rochester, NY: Camden House.

Pawel, E. (1984). *The nightmare of reason*. New York: Farrar, Straus, and Giroux.

Prose, F. (2006). Close reading. *The Atlantic: Fiction Issue 2006,* 8–11.

Rigney, B. H. (1978). *Madness and sexual politics in the feminist novels: Studies in Bronte, Woolf, Lessing, and Atwood*. Madison: The University of Wisconsin Press.

Rosenblatt, L. (1995). *Literature as exploration*. 5th ed. New York: The Modern Language Association of America.

Scheele, A. (2004, May 6). The good student trap. *Washington Post*. Retrieved May 10, 2004, from: http://www.washingtonpost.com.

Sillers, P. (1979). Power impinging: Hearing Atwood's vision. *Studies in Canadian Literature, 4* (1). Retrieved October 9, 2006, at http://www.lib.unb.ca/Texts/SCL/bin/get.cgi?directory=v014_1/&filename=sillers.htm.

Snell, M. (1997, July/August). Margaret Atwood. *Mother Jones.*

Stein, K. F. (1999). *Margaret Atwood revisited*. New York: Twayne.

Thomas, P. L. (1998, March). "It beckons, and it baffles—": Resurrecting Emily Dickinson (and poetry) in the student-centered classroom. *English Journal, 87* (3), 60–63.

Thomas, P. (2001). *Lou LaBrant: A woman's life, a teacher's life*. Huntington, NY: Nova Science.

Thomas, P. L. (2004). *Numbers games: Measuring and mandating American education*. New York: Peter Lang.

Thomas, P. L. (2005a). *Reading, learning, teaching Barbara Kingsolver*. New York: Peter Lang.

Thomas, P. L. (2006). *Reading, learning, teaching Kurt Vonnegut*. New York: Peter Lang.

Thomas, P. L. (2005b). *Teaching writing primer.* New York: Peter Lang.

VanSpanckeren, K., & Castro, J. G., eds. (1988). *Margaret Atwood: Vision and forms.* Carbondale: Southern Illinois University Press.

Vonnegut, K. (2005). *A man without a country.* New York: Seven Stories.

Vonnegut, K. (1974). *Wampeters, foma, & granfalloons.* New York: Delta.

Wagner-Martin, L. (1994). *Telling women's lives: The new biography.* New Brunswick, NJ: Rutgers University Press.

Weaver, C. (1996). *Teaching grammar in context.* Portsmouth, NH: Boynton/Cook.

Wilson, M. (2006, Spring). Apologies to Sandra Cisneros. *Rethinking Schools, 20* (3), 42–46.

Wilson, M. (2006). *Rethinking rubrics in writing assessment.* Portsmouth, NH: Heinemann.

Wilson, S. R., ed. (2003). *Margaret Atwood's textual assassinations: Recent poetry and fiction.* Columbus: The Ohio State University Press.

Wilson, S. R., Friedman, T. B., & Hengen, S. (1996). *Approaches to teaching Atwood's* The Handmaid's Tale *and other works.* New York: The Modern Language Association of America.

Woolf, V. (1991). *A room of one's own.* New York: Harcourt.

Zinsser, W. (2001). *On writing well: The classic guide to writing nonfiction.* 25th Anniversary Ed. New York: Quill/ A Harper Resource.